Advance Praise for *World Gone [Beautiful]*

Reading this book, I'm struck by how studied
ered the pursuit of peace can be—how earnestly we desire
it—and yet how that peace seems to reveal itself most when
the mind is stilled and the searcher has paused. In this book,
in the matrices between these keenly observed and deeply
felt labors, there are great threads and ribbons of luminosity.
World Gone Beautiful is a lovely work, well-rendered, and as
honest as the day is long.
—Rick Bass, *The Lives of Rocks* and *The Ninemile Wolves*

The trick with memoir is whether or not the reader is invited
into a neighborhood that seems friendly. Reading Linda
Buturian's remembering is like having a cup of tea on an
unwinding day with a few folks that you really like. This
neighborhood is friendly indeed.
—Dale Brown, *Of Faith and Fiction* and *Conversations with
American Writers*

In *World Gone Beautiful*, Linda Buturian introduces us to
the contemporary ascesis of intentional living, of deliberate
faith, and of the choice to become a member of the Body,
truly. She reminds me that, as the fathers say, we are all
called to martyrdom; and she reminds me that, so long as
we're doing it, we should seek to do it beautifully.
—Scott Cairns, *Short Trip to the Edge* and *Compass of
Affection*

Linda Buturian's prose is as beautiful as the lives and homes she seeks to evoke. Alert, honest, and painstaking, Buturian dwells in stubborn affection for her land and neighbors in rural Minnesota. To read her is to step into community that lasts.

—Paul J. Willis, *Bright Shoots of Everlastingness*

Rarely has a book been named more perfectly than Linda Buturian's *World Gone Beautiful*. Every kind of beauty—of nature, of family, of neighbor and the spirit—illuminates this rich, funny, deeply felt book. Nothing seems to escape Buturian's fresh gaze, and in the wideness of her vision, the world we thought we knew is commented on, understood, and transformed.

—Erin McGraw, *The Good Life*, and *The Seamstress of Hollywood Boulevard*

World Gone Beautiful is a scouting report from a necessary American future where people are learning to do more with less. Linda Buturian's writing, like the "intentional cul-de-sac" she inhabits and celebrates, is nurturing yet edgy, serene yet surprising, good-hearted but dead-honest, idyllic yet raw, reverent *and* (thank God!) irreverent. This book satisfies like a walk by a river, a fine book of poems, or the oddball neighbor who, you realize over time, has become a cherished friend.

—David James Duncan, *The Brothers K* and *God Laughs and Plays*

World Gone Beautiful

Amy ~

Seeing You Again is
A Harbinger of
Our World Gone Beautiful.

Blessings.

~ Linda 2008

World Gone Beautiful

Life Along the Rum River

Linda Buturian

Cathedral Hill Press
St. Paul, Minnesota

Portions of essays have appeared in *OE Journal* and *Mille Lacs Messenger*. Mentioned: "Beyond the Bale" *Utne Reader* September/October 1997. Anne Lamott interviews. *Utne Reader, The OE Journal, Shouts and Whispers: Twenty-One Writers Speak About Their Writing and Their Faith* edited by Jennifer L. Holberg (Eerdmans 2006). Interviews with John Peyton, Fran Blacklock, and Hudson are available upon request at www.LindaButurian.com

Cover art by Jim Larson

Cathedral Hill Press, 1043 Grand Ave #213, St. Paul MN, 55105
Printed in the United States on acid-free paper

Library of Congress Cataloging-in-Publication Data
Buturian, Linda, 1962-
World gone beautiful : life along the Rum River / Linda Buturian.
   p. cm.
ISBN 978-0-9742986-3-4 (alk. paper)
1. Buturian, Linda, 1962- 2. Buturian, Linda, 1962—Family. 3. Country life—Minnesota—Bogus Brook Township. 4. Country life—Minnesota—Rum River Region (River) 5. Community life—Minnesota—Bogus Brook Township. 6. Community life—Minnesota—Rum River Region (River) 7. Bogus Brook Township (Minn.)—Social life and customs. 8. Rum River Region (Minn. : River)—Social life and customs. 9. Bogus Brook Township (Minn.)—Description and travel. 10. Rum River Region (Minn. : River)—Description and travel. I. Title.
F614.B64B88 2008
977.6'68—dc22

2008003907

Contents

Directions   12

Great Bird   16

The Secret Pond   38

Inherited Beauty   68

Buddha in the Compost   92

Dostoevsky on the Rum   120

Henry Bird and the Dogs of Bogus Brook   142

Acknowledgments   168

Dedicated to my grandmothers~
Sophia Buturian and Adeline Colasurd.

Then he said, not so lightly, "You get into things, you know. You sort of don't realize what you're getting into."
—*Alice Munro quoting her father,*
The View from Castle Rock

A good samurai will parry the blow.
—*Helen Dewitt, The Last Samurai*

We may be brothers after all.
We will see.
—*Attributed to Chief Seattle,*
translated by Dr. Henry Smith, 1854

Directions

When you drive down County Road 4 in Bogus Brook Township, turn onto a tree-lined gravel road marked by a yellow Dead End sign. If you are in a dark or speculative mood you might interpret that sign as a message about our lives (or your own). Keep going, past the black and white Holsteins taking shade under the poplars. If the neighbor hasn't just spread liquid manure on his field, roll down your window to get a glimpse of the wild pink geraniums blooming in the ditch, and to hear the frogs before they cease all at once as you pass their marsh, and pick up again only when you are driving along the cornfields. Flickers appear to be guiding your car as they arc from tree to tree, flashing their white rump feathers. A deer, possum, or fox might cross your path. The road turns into our gravel drive and you see my house beyond the hayfield, with stucco walls and wood siding (the Larsons'). The drive leads you to the farmhouse with its wraparound porch and swing, home to my husband's brother and his family (also the Larsons'). The seven of us who bought the property together twelve years ago shared the farmhouse. We're friends who wanted to live by each other and could afford the land together. It continues to make good sense.

By now the dogs are announcing your arrival, the littlest one running and jumping on your car. Someone should do something about that. Cats are hiding and aware of your presence. Drive past the only substantial concrete around—a half-court with a basketball hoop, a green tennis wall, and skateboard ramp—and then you are facing a long building that makes you put on your brakes. Is it a barn? A garage? It has been both and now the two-story red-sided building with white trim is the home and shop of the Munsons'. Press on past the gardens and the wood-fired hot tub and the yellow playhouse that used to be blue and in a tree, to where the drive ends at a timber framed straw-bale house (the Larsons', again). Note the lone horse grazing in the field. Hidden from sight, beyond the sweep of meadows and trees, flows the wild Rum River.

Living: 4 houses, 8 adults, 7 kids, 4 dogs, 6 cats, 1 horse.
Dead: 2 dogs, 1 horse, 1 canary, 25 chickens, Grandpa Don.

You could walk the trails that loop around our property down through the meadows and along the woods by the river. When you circle back, the trail curves and your gaze is directed to a view of the houses, so it's easy to miss the deer path obscured by tall grasses. Ten wet steps through goldenrod and Joe-pye weed and you would have been in a dip of earth teeming with rocks. Some call it the quarry, others the rock pile. A giant bowl of stones ringed by trees, scattered with rusting remains of farm implements—spoked wheel, yoke, tractor seat, discs, a roll of barbed wire. Most likely the quarry was a dumping place for farmers who for decades pulled stones from the fields, but someone once suggested that the river used to run through here. In the quarry you feel hidden, though you are close enough to the houses your shout could be heard. It is a good place to go when you need to think, or need help setting thinking aside. The heat from the rocks on your legs is a comfort, and you are surrounded by flecked, banded, speckled, vesicular, helmet-sized, anvil-squared, prehistoric-egg shaped granite, basalt, jasper, lava, rhyolite, and sandstone.

With the tractor we've hauled up rocks to border our gardens. When a retaining wall was being made and I could hear the rumble of the tractor for days, I worried that we would run out, but then I walked down to the quarry and it looked as if no stone was touched. The rocks are infinite, it seems, and changing at such an unhurried pace as if to slow down even time.

Great Bird

(2005)

"Toss in some sunflowers and millet and make sure there's water." Jonathan hands me the black wire cage, the olive canary flitting from perch to side, the sun bright on the street where we agreed to meet. "Give 'em a piece of lettuce or whatever you're cooking. He likes that." I want to kiss Jonathan even though there are beads of sweat on his upper lip, I'm not attracted to him, I'm married, and my girls are hovering around the cage. What is it about recently divorced men that makes me want to gather them to my breast and reassure them that their worst fear of themselves isn't the only truth?

The metal handle digs into my palm as I watch Jonathan walk to the car. *I'm sorry for your loss. It'll be okay. Maybe even better.* His body language and brusque tone chuffs off any talk of the personal, of the flames around him. Reach for him and you'll burn. "Oh yeah," he turns. "Ozzy likes flyin' around the house but don't let him outside. He'll never make it."

"I'll take good care of your bird Jonathan." Buckling the girls in their car seats, I adjust the cage between them and start the seventy mile drive back to our place in the country, mulling over this affinity for divorced men. When I was eight, Mom divorced Dad and he moved across town into a dingy apartment and got depressed. Before we would go over to see him, Mom would say, "Cheer up your dad. Put some art on the walls. Help him make dinner." The thought is a flare lighting up the dark hall of memory.

I glance in the mirror at the girls watching Ozzy bob like a castaway on a lifeboat.

"Did I ever tell you about when my little brother was seven and he crocheted our dad an afghan out of red and black yarn?"

"What is crochet?" Audrey, four, asks.

"A kind of knitting. J.D. wanted it big enough to cover our Dad. He worked on it for two years and gave it to Dad the second Christmas. We took turns cuddling up in it on the couch."

"Mom can we hold the birdie?" asks Franny, two and a half, who has her finger on the cage, her blue eyes intent on the bird's frantic movements. Audrey's brown eyes are watching me watch Franny.

"It would make her—I mean him—too nervous."

"Well what can we do with him?"

Pull over and deposit him on the curb. "We can find our own name for him."

"What's wrong with Ozzy?" says Audrey. "I like the name."

"Ozzy is named after the rock singer Ozzy Osbourne. When he was on stage he would bite the heads off of canaries and spit them out."

Their eyes widen and stare at me to make sure I'm not joking. "That's mean," Audrey says.

We settle on Goldie, even though the bird is not canary yellow, but a drab olive with a bright tuft of gold. As tall buildings and strip malls morph into housing developments and flat squares of farmland, the buzzing steps up in my head. What was I thinking of, taking this bird? I am entranced by ideas. The idea is so shiny and full of promise. The idea of the bird sounded so good and then there's bird crap and feeding and lurking death. This is how I live my life. Somehow I manage to hold down a full-time job, stay married ten years, raise my kids, tend to a house in the country, and live in a community with three other families—all good ideas I chose—but the living out of these ideas makes me feel weak-hearted in the world. When I'm drying dishes and staring out at the dark field, Dylan's line surfaces, "Vaguely sensing she's caught." I'm thinking someone should give me a medal, a ribbon even, for staying put, for holding a life together.

"He looks like a sparrow," my husband Jeff proclaims as he props up the large cage in the living room. He means a House Sparrow and this is the lowest thing you could say about a bird in our community. For nine years now, we have all lived on a hundred acres in the country along the Rum River, and we've seen how House Sparrows take over native song birds' nesting sites. Jeff's brother Brett and his wife Diane (M.S. specializing in ornithology) have a trap that catches House Sparrows. At my feeders on the days when there are only House Sparrows I think why am I feeding the CEOs of Wal-Mart and Halliburton?

We prop up the cage door and wait. All morning Goldie is silent, but by the afternoon his beautiful trills fill up our vaulted room. It pleases me that the bird matches our olive and wheat painted walls. We carry his cage out to the porch and he flies from screen to screen then lands on top of the cage and stays there for a long time, until we leave him alone and when we walk in again he's settled back in and life feels fine.

In the living room, Goldie hops from the hutch to the couch, flies to the sink and pecks on the formica. I call our beagle Sadie over and pet her soft brown ears as she watches Goldie hop along the floor. I explain this is an Inside Bird and part of our clan now and she can't eat it or paw it. Sadie's lids around her brown eyes make her look like she has eyeliner on and she gives me a withering gaze that reminds me of my Italian grandmother: *You're kidding. First babies, now this.* She retreats to her bed in protest.

The kids in the community come to check out the bird. Along with our two, there are seven. Eight-year-old Miles (Alpha male of the clan), studies Goldie with his intent blue eyes. "I think it's cool you have a bird in the house. It's like bringing nature inside. Did you know that peregrine falcons can fly vertically as fast as two hundred miles per hour?" Miles may one day be our president or design a car that runs on sound. His little sister Olivia sings a song to Goldie, then says, "I think she's lonely."

The thought drops into my head like a parachuter releasing her balloon. This is a bird that lost his bird-father three years ago, lost his female caregiver when the marriage devolved, and just lost Jonathan. Is he lonely? I worry that my little Franny is left out of the older kids' games, that my husband is lonely even in community, and now my worry-lasso has caught this bird.

"Do you think Goldie is lonely?" I ask Jeff, who's washing radishes, his calves big like Belgian horses', dusted with dirt from the garden.

"Birds don't have emotions."

"But we really don't know whether it's lonely. Birds are not like dogs. They are wholly other; I have no sense of his internal life."

Jeff hands me a plump radish. Though I won't eat it, I like the heft of it in my hand, the radiance of the red skin contrasting with black flecks of dirt. "Bird brain, remember? He doesn't have an internal life. Let's worry about what we're going to have for dinner. That bird's got it great here. Bet he didn't fly much at Jonathan's."

Brett wanders over from the farmhouse we all shared nine years ago, and squints in the cage. "He looks like a sparrow." For Brett's insult I hand him a can of Grain Belt Beer instead of a Summit. I show him the picture in the canary book of how Goldie actually looks like his wild forbears, olive, with a mustard yellow sheen. "It's not an insult," he adds. "I like sparrows. Just not House Sparrows."

The next day I leave Audrey and her cousin Leif, six, in the house while I run next door, warning them, "Do not go on the porch, Do not open the cage, Do not touch the bird." Leif has spiky white-blond hair and blue eyes and is a great kid who now and again can look like a cherub while he lies through his teeth; Audrey is a first-born rule keeper and rarely disobeys me. A few minutes later, from my neighbor Cyndy's yard, I glance over to see the kids in the porch, see the dark shape of the bird in the air. I run back to find Goldie lying on the cage floor, convulsing, his claws curled up, Leif standing next to him. I double over in automatic weeping, turn Goldie on his stomach where he lies splayed, heartbeat spasming his little body. I shove Leif on the couch and Audrey on the chair and both start crying loud and hard.

"What did you do?" I put my finger in Leif's face. "You killed him. You killed my bird. Why didn't you listen to me?" Leif and Audrey have never seen me like this.

Leif's face is bright red as he wails, "I didn't hear you!" Which makes me more furious.

"You killed my bird. And now you're lying to me."

"I didn't mean to!"

Audrey weeps, holds out her arms to me.

"You stay here." As I run over to Cyndy's I imagine telling Jonathan I killed his bird after only two days, which makes me cry harder. Cyndy comes back and comforts the kids and cups Goldie in her hands and strokes him, saying calmly, "I think he'll make it."

It turns out Leif had seen a TV show where a trainer released a falcon, so he decided to try it. The first time went great—he tossed Goldie up and he flew around the porch. The second toss was too hard and Goldie hit the ceiling and dropped to the floor.

The rest of the day Goldie stands on his perch, breathing fast and shallow, eyes bright, the essence of fear. The air is filled with terror now. I lie awake and picture Goldie slamming against the ceiling. I think about how, when you let something fly, you release it into danger (a plane, a marriage, a child, your words, your love for someone). And how Leif will now think I am the witchiest woman in community. Medusa, the Cruella de Ville of the Compound. He will always look at me with a bit of fear.

"The mind rushes on, a drunk elephant" says Kabir. I look over and watch Jeff who, like a soldier, sleeps instantly and deeply when and where he can. The irony is that I, an insomniac, would marry the world's best sleeper. He is America and I am Haiti and night after night I look over hungrily. I have P.M.S. and it is three in the morning and the world is a model airplane I must assemble in the dark, without instructions. I am holding the universe together with the glue of my worry. I toss and turn on our new king size bed, which I thought would be the Shangri-La of my sleep problems, only I read an article about off-gassing from beds made of synthetic materials and since we've gotten it I've woken up with puffy eyes and wheezing breath, and in this moment, the bed seems like a toxic island, like a cancer machine, like—

"Honey," I nudge him, "Jeff."

"Huh. Which kid's awake."

"I'm sorry. I'm freaking out. I think this bed is going to give us cancer. And I saw this mother being really mean to her kids in the grocery store, and it got me thinking about kids and abuse and why do we live out here and how Audrey's going to end up pregnant by a four-wheeling, tobacco-chewing, camo-wearing, gun-toting emotionally frozen son. I want to get rid of Goldie, sell the cars, why did we build such a big house? And we're committed to the community and have no exit plan. How can we sell even if we wanted to move? We used to live in a VW Van for God's sake, now look at us. We both have to work full time, we're tired and grouchy and—"

"Here," Jeff holds out his hand. His large Swedish face looks moonish at night.

"What."

"It's a 'Get Out Of Your Brain Free' card. Take it."

I giggle. He's never thought of that before.

"Come here." I lean into his broad warm body and he puts his strong arms around me. "It'll be alright. We can't leave right now. Give into that. But if you really, really keep wanting to leave, we'll find a way." I find my breathing with his and start to feel my brain recede like a tide. "Look," he adds. "I've woken up kinda wheezy too, but it'll pass. We'll open up the windows and let the bed air out ... Hey, now that we're awake do you wanna have sex?"

In the morning I call Leif and apologize for yelling. Later, a note appears in my mailbox in spidery boy writing. "Sorry I hurt yer bird. And din't lisen to you. Leif." He drew a rather good likeness of Goldie. Leif rides over on his bike and plays with the girls like nothing ever happened.

Another day passes before Goldie hops to the hutch, flutters to the couch, and flies back to the top of the cage. His song finds us in the house; I watch Jeff watching the bird, listening.

The afternoon sun shines in as I sit cross-legged in the green Lazy Boy grading papers a few feet away from Goldie. When he sings I can see his whole body working to make those complicated trills. One layer of melody is like a teeny Pavarotti, and below that are Africans singing three different sounds simultaneously. Time stops and it is an exquisite pleasure to be so close to his pulsating throat, his shiny eye, his song. Every time the phone rings he starts up again. I want people to call just to make him sing, but after a while Jeff is hollering, "Shut up already!" God gives us paradise and we tire of the vivid blues, the intense greens, the buzzing of cicadas.

On the Greensprings in the mountains of Oregon, when I was in my early twenties, I would visit my theology professor in his old wood house. John would be slouched on the couch, his black knit cap over his flaking hair, talking about something like the Hebrew word *nefesh* in the book of Genesis, translated variously as God's throat, the place where life begins, the breath that animals and humans share, what animates us. *Nefesh* is also used to refer to the living creatures before humans. When God shapes the dust and breathes into it, it too becomes alive. The TV would be on, John's wife Nancy would move in and out of the room, pausing to add her insights, flipping her long black hair, smiling at me, handing me a slice of warm bread, their two daughters rolling toys in, drawing me pictures, their Sheltie yapping every time someone in their community walked by. And all the while, Nancy's lovebirds would be flying through the house, from bookshelf to plant—a hurtling yellow, a blue flutter of wings—and I would feel known in this chaos. Fifteen years later I have created my own rendition of that lovely chaos.

"Get that bird outta here!" Jeff hollers from the kitchen, swinging at the bird. "We're all gonna die of encephalitis." Goldie dive bombs Jeff especially, grazing his ear, and then he lights on the top of our kitchen cupboards and cocks his head and peers down at Jeff. A blur of wings and rapid chirping then Goldie settles into his cage.

Audrey slides down the cage door. "Even though Dad is yelling at the bird he still likes Goldie."

"I do not."

"Yes you do Dad. You love Goldie." Audrey the firstborn, narrating the unwritten script for our family roles.

"Birds belong outside." Jeff flips the burgers and lifts the lid to the steaming broccoli.

"She would die outside Jonathan said."

"He," Audrey corrects me.

"Good." Jeff cuts a thick slice of his warm oatmeal-wheat bread, and spreads more butter than I would let myself, and hands it to me.

Months slide by. Our life with Goldie takes on a rhythm. I open the cage door and let him fly whenever I'm around. We have a giant moose antler Jeff found in the North woods, propped up on top of the kitchen cupboards and Goldie loves to perch on it, like it's the tallest tree branch in his terrain. He hops around on the kitchen island while the girls color, cocks his head at me, and chirps like he's narrating our lives, and I remember that I had a robin for a pet. We called it Robbie and Mom let us take it in the car all the way from Ohio to Tennessee where she had scored a free getaway for her and us four kids. Robbie sat on my lap in the backseat in a styrofoam to-go box, and we would let it hop around at rest stops. We had that bird until it died in the garage, most likely from asphyxiation. Mom found it in the morning when she was getting in the car to go to work, and she cried. The only time Mom ever cried was when she watched *Born Free* or a pet died.

One day I am sitting in the living room and Goldie is hopping across the floor and Sadie leaps up and pounces, like some ancient hunting instinct resurrected itself before her brain woke up. She lifts a paw and —

"*No*," I holler and grab her collar and put her in the down position and immediately she is ashamed. Goldie hops over as I'm rubbing Sadie's stomach, and I am thinking how much I just like Sadie, how she's been with me from the start of our marriage, and how I can tell what she's feeling all the time, which is comforting to me. This bird is an enigma.

Sometimes when I prop the cage door up and press it against the cage to secure it, the door slams back down. Goldie jumps away in time, taken aback. I rush over and open it more carefully. Other times the kids will be jumping so hard it shuts the cage door when he's out and then he can't get back in. I make a mental note to put a latch on the door in order to keep it open

"That's it. It's the bird or me." Jeff is standing on a chair peering over the top of our cupboards. He's a big Swede so he looks like a giant. I get up there and understand why he is making that gagging sound like he's going to heave. The top of the cupboards is splattered with birdcrap. It looks like Central Park after an old lady tossed out bread crumbs. It is revolting, perched right there above our food-lives. "That bird has got to fly less." I grab soapy water and a sponge and somehow the gluey texture of the poop and the rough pressboard makes it impossible to clean. I climb down and still it hovers there.

At five thirty in the morning I haven't even turned the coffeepot on and the bird starts chirping. Goldie will not stop until I put in some seed and prop open the cage door. And even then he has to talk to me like we're two old people swapping accounts of how bad we slept (I woke up thirteen times. My back is killing me. Chirp-chirp). I come home after teaching at the university—one-and-a-half to two hours in commute—and walk through the door to the dog wagging her tail with a stuffed animal in her mouth, the bird chirping madly, scuttling back and forth on the poop-filled newspaper because of course Jeff never let her out, the girls both needing me, and Jeff asking logistical questions about bills and dinner and did I remember cream and—. It makes me understand the old farmwife mentality of "one more mouth to feed." It all comes down to feeding, clothing, and excrement. I decide I'm gonna give that bird up. I write the ad in my head:

> Needs home: Canary that looks like a sparrow. Must fly every day. Sings like Callas, shits like a newborn.

One day Miles and Olivia's cat got in the house. Jingles is a sleek black panther freed of any social constraints. He lunges at your legs and climbs up curtains and moves like a stud, looking for a new lay. The kids were running in and out of the downstairs back door, and the cat must have slipped in. All I know is I'm sitting on the living room carpet and this black cat struts by licking his lips, like in the cartoons, and I look up at the empty bird cage, door propped open, and think there's that then. I walk through the house yodeling, "Goldie. Yoo-hoo. Goldie-bird." Six kids are running around and I tell them the first one to find the bird gets a quarter. Goldie! Goldie!

No sign of him, but neither of carnage—there would be feathers and bones. I am noticing, next to sadness, a pint of relief. It would be nice to be free of this little shitter. It would be one less thing to clean up after and to annoy Jeff and—"Found him!" Leif holds up his palm for the quarter; Goldie is downstairs tucked up in the ductwork, hiding from the chaos of the kids.

It is late winter in Minnesota. The house is closing in on me. I am weary of rising above: rising above the desire to lay down in the middle of the day, to have a drink in one hand and the remote in the other, of wanting to play with my friends, to do one thing, just one thing at a time, whether it's read to Franny or watch Audrey's gymnastics or listen to Jeff's account of his day or pet Sadie, but not all of these at once, please.

I am washing out the green plastic compost bucket which I had hurled out the front door and left for a month in protest of winter. The hot water has warmed the frozen food and the odor makes me swoon. I put a new charcoal filter in the lid, and scatter some baking soda on the bottom. Jeff comes in from feeding the chickens and I announce proudly that the compost is back in action.

"Until it sits out in the snow for another two months."

On another day I would have giggled, but at this moment in my mind I hiss, "I hate you." It's not personal. It is the ongoing cold war that marriage becomes. The thousand details that nickel and dime away the dowry of our love. The constant barrage of needs from two young children, two cars, two jobs, a house, a community, so that we have no buoyancy, so that when I need him to say, "You're doing a great job honey," and instead he says, "Why do you have to pile everything on the counter right where I need to roll out the dough," or I want him to tell me, "You're a good mother," and what comes out of his mouth is, "The kids never learn consequences. You don't make them clean up." And when his back is spasming, the dead last thing I want to do is to stop my spinning (folding up clothes, shaking out dog-hair rugs, grading sixty-five papers), and give him a massage. And I know, by the look he gives me, that he hates me too in the moment, though the entirety of his life will not allow him to admit such a feeling. And I know that this is going on in homes across America—good loving people—my neighbors included. I have seen couples in Target where the wife is holding out a purchase and talking to her husband in a clipped, overly polite way, as if he were a client she loathed but whose business she needed to keep, and the husband is looking away from her, his words escaping from a closed mouth, his face a mask of the cold war.

A veteran of his childhood, Jeff emerges at times judgmental and defensive. I say something and he bites back in a way that alerts me that he has confused me with his mother or his father. In response I become an unattractive blend of castrating and victimish, and he becomes the source of all of my unhappiness. I talk to him through gritted teeth, he pounds out of the room. One time we were in the car tussling about who should go in and return some movies. I stayed in the car while he stormed in. Audrey asks, "Mom, are you mad at Dad?" Yes. "Why did you marry him if you don't like him?"

A few days later, Franny and the neighbor Louis are playing, and it is getting close to when I drive them to preschool. I open the cage door to give Goldie a chance for a brief spin, walk away, hear the door slam, and turn to see Goldie flailing. The door, now a guillotine, seems to have broken her back. I rush over, cup the bird in my hands, knowing she's a goner. "I killed my bird. I killed my bird," I moan over and over. I sit on the green Lazy Boy as two three-year-olds hover around. Louis reassures me that Goldie is sleepy and I should put him back in the cage. Franny pets him gently as we watch Goldie go from struggle to relent, watch the natural forces taking over, his shiny dot of an eye closing, closing. I feel his heat move into my hands. Franny holds my arm. I wish I could stop crying. When he is dead I call my neighbor and sister-in-law Diane, whom I always call for bird troubles (hummingbird trapped in garage, bluebird diving into window). She puts Goldie in a shoebox on the porch and helps me buckle the kids in the car.

As I drive, I keep glancing at Franny in the rearview mirror. She is smiling and talking to Louis and doesn't seem affected. After I drop them off I wander around the small town of Princeton feeling deranged (me an environmentalist animal lover, causing the death of a bird). I drift into the balloon shop for Audrey's upcoming birthday party, and blurt out to the lady that my bird just died. She looks away and I feel like some prattling hormonally challenged woman, then she says, "Well, so are you thinking of a kind of ceremony, so something in black perhaps?" I laugh no, explain about Audrey's party. "Well if you do have a ceremony, you could let a balloon go to help the kids understand about death. And the latex isn't a problem for birds; they aren't interested in biting it. It's the string that's troublesome, so you could cut it right before you let the balloon go." I walk out with two gold helium balloons.

When Audrey and Cedar and Olivia come home from school, Franny and I break the news and hug Audrey as her little face crumples up. She cries hard, then opens the shoebox and the girls take turns holding Goldie. They pry open his eyelids, tug on the claws, extend the wings, and pet him boldly. They do in death what they couldn't in life. We talk about souls and heaven. I explain how Goldie's body is here, but his spirit is somewhere else. This is their first glimpse at death and this paradox seems clunky and unsatisfying, but the girls accept it with the easy grace that only children can. Cedar says, "Maybe the balloon knows where Goldie's spirit is, and so wherever the balloon goes, there goes Goldie."

Brett stops over with two Grain Belts. No one blames me for the bird because I don't need any help putting on that crown of thorns. When Jeff gets home he digs a hole in the still-frozen front yard. Our family gathers around the hole with the shoebox and the balloons. We say a prayer and tell Goldie we love him. I cut the strings and we watch the gold balloons drifting in circles up into the grey sky. I am surprised when Franny says she wants to be the one to put Goldie in the hole. She takes him out of the box, stares at his little body, then the dark soil, then puts him in and starts crying. Good-bye great bird.

We head in. The empty cage looms in the corner. Jeff

heats up leftover turkey, and I am relieved the girls don't make the connection. He hands Franny and Audrey their first wishbone, which he had been drying on the sill. "Now make a wish and pull and your wish will come true." Audrey gets the larger piece.

"What was your wish Franny?"

She looks small in her too-tight favorite red velvet pants and cowgirl boots, holding the short end of the bone. "I wished God and Jesus and Mary and their donkey Whisper would sit at our table and eat dinner with us." Her blue eyes are trained on Jeff. "You were wrong. My wish didn't come true. God's not here."

Jeff and I look at each other. He says, "Maybe one day your wish will come true."

"Some people say God is here right now," I add.

"But I want to see him," Franny insists.

"Maybe God is a she." As we eat turkey we all chime in on whether God is a he or a she or a he-she, or perhaps a tiger. As we are clearing the dishes, the energy turns and Jeff and I start in. I say something hard and he retreats to the bedroom. Franny looks up from her coloring. "You can't get mad at God."

"Do you think God looks like Jeff?"

"Yes, only skinny."

"Should we draw God so you can show me?"

Jeff comes back in and we take a break from the cold

war and sit around the table, drawing pictures of God. Franny draws him in brown crayon with long hair and holding his arms out, surrounded by a rainbow and blue people flying all around him. "He's thinking of us," she says. "He's using his imagination. This is Cedar holding Goldie dead, and in her other hand she's holding a dead goldfinch; that's why the bird is dark, cuz he was laying down in the dirt. Cedar's starting a bird collection and she's going to give them to God."

The cold war is not what surprises me anymore. It is that love keeps finding us. That Fortuna's wheel circles away from hatred or disdain back to ease and intimacy. I remember my professor John talking about how sometimes the status quo can be a sign of grace. Back then, when I had no desire for a normal life, that idea lodged in my mind, and it finds me now that I have become, in many ways, the status quo. Love finds me here.

The Secret Pond

(2007)

In the morning when all things still feel possible, and the coffee and cream is just-right-hot in my blue mug, I turn on the computer. As I wait for it to go through parallel motions of yawning and getting out of bed, I glance out the screen porch past the poplars to check on my neighbors, noting the flicker of the TV at the farmhouse and the sleepy state of the strawbale dwelling, and just down the path I see Dana preparing to put up board and batten siding on the renovated barn. Yesterday he stained red the pine boards and narrow battens, and they are lined up on carpenter horses. I sit back down at the table, read what I'd written the day before, revise, and write a few more pages. I stare and think. I get up, eat a handful of nuts, fill my water glass, wander around, and look out the window to see Dana has sided a third of the wall. Go back to the computer, labor over a paragraph, draft more, walk outside to dump the compost and fill the feeder and note the mostly finished wall. By the day's end he has also trimmed the window with broad white boards. It is hard not to compare my pages of words that might engage and edify some readers to Dana's handsome, functional siding that will protect his family and resist Minnesota winters.

Over the eleven years Dana and I have lived alongside each other, I've written a couple of stories, essays, columns, interviews, and plodded on with a novel, all accompanied by the rumble of the tractor as Dana has hauled bucket loads of river rock for a retaining wall, moved his many piles of wood, and plowed the drive. I've graded papers and prepared lectures for teaching to the sound of sawing and hammering as he framed in doors, and baled and stuccoed walls. I don't need Chairman Mao to help me determine whose work seems to have more value. Dana's end product is obvious and useful; mine is invisible, and then occasionally becomes visible in print. I cycle back to the old questions: Why write? Why do anything that's not entirely utilitarian? With age and an awareness of a volition not entirely my own, I've come to accept that writing is one of the things I do.

At least I'm not alone. Of the eight adults living here, half of us are often writing. Late at night when I'm working it is comforting to look out at the neighbors' lights and picture them drafting a sermon or newspaper article or grant. In the same way you can find a car around here when you need to borrow one, you can always track someone down to read and edit your work.

I walk out the screen porch to the backyard and hear my eight-year-old nephew Leif holler, "Look at me!" His voice isn't coming from the swing-set or a bike on the loop of gravel drive. "Up here!" I shield my eyes from the sun and see a dark form near the top of the tallest poplar in the cluster by our propane tank. Leif's blonde hair is backlit as the tree sways back and forth like in those cartoons when a bear is caught up on the thinnest branches.

"Amazing Leif. Now *get down*! It's too high!"

He scrambles down, ecstatic, legs and arms scratched up, and I tell him he can't climb that again without his mom or dad watching. A few hours later he brings Diane over, and while he starts up she and I stand in the driveway sipping wine, remembering to check his progress now and again, and then Diane's eyes press out and she shouts in a cracking voice I've rarely heard out of her, "*Leif* Larson you *get down* here *right now* that is *way too high."* Leif is about half as far as he was the first time.

Leif, aptly named for the explorer, marked out new terrain. In my mind the poplars now bear the imprint of his impression. Kids are like moving stories: they create new ways of being through their words, actions and expressions. Miles and Cedar came along first and were born within a few weeks of each other. Both had traumatic births in different parts of the states, and both nearly died before they had a chance at living. My experience of the poplars has absorbed Leif swinging near the top, and my relationships to Cedar and Miles contain gazing down at them when they were on ventilators, and willing them to live through prayers and technology. They have healthy, happy lives, and mostly I don't think about their beginnings, but now and again they surface in my mind and remind me of what is true for all of the children—their presence is a gift.

The kids help me to see things slant. Olivia and Audrey were about four or five, and it was early winter when Olivia showed up at the door in a new fluffy pink coat. Audrey asked, "Oh, is that made out of wool?" Olivia said, "No, it's made out of winter." The other day Franny, six, asked, "Mom, when they sing 'It's a small world after all,' is that a compliment to the world or are they saying to God that they want a bigger place?" In between these comments are swaths of time consumed with the daily tedium of making snacks and negotiating for more media, but when these moments come along, I am like a worker on a plantation sucking on sugar cane; while I move through the field of my day I chew on their words to revive the sweetness.

On some level I feel like I am one of the kids because what I most like to do in the world is to hear stories. These past ten years while living on the land, whether inserting ads in newspapers at the printing press, helping seniors draw up Living Wills, or teaching in college, I was listening; especially to old people. As if life is one long conveyor belt that moves in a looping, halting-forward fashion, I see a certain old person ahead, and run to catch up, "Wait, before you get much further along, step aside, tell me what you've seen, how you've spent your time."

Back when we had just moved here and were sharing the farmhouse, I received a grant to interview ninety-year-old artist and writer John Peyton, who lived outside of Duluth. It turned out to be the first of several interviews I had with older Minnesotans. I had seen John give a slide show of his watercolors, and read some of the five books he wrote and illustrated in his eighties. I was drawn to his art, his sensibility, his respect for the Northwoods Indians he grew up with. Though he was ninety, I was slightly in love with him. His sense of wonder was alive and he had these tufts of eyebrows that moved with a will of their own over his steady grey eyes. When he quoted Tennyson's "Deep Bones Round," it was as if the poem about mortality was revealing his heart's own thoughts. At the time John was busy working on three different books, one on computer art, which he had recently taught himself and embraced as a tool for creating.

Aside from his years at Yale and studying with New York painters, John lived in his hometown of Proctor, where I met with him. We talked in John's office in his daughter's home, and drove out to see the cabin he had built in the twenties with his wife, Fay, who was an artist and dancer. He hadn't lived in the cabin for years. Dust covered the wall length mirror that Fay bought from a saloon, and the shelves of books still lining the living room. While John hunted for a specific title, he told me about Fay teaching their kids and friends her choreographed dances. They made money for a while hatching goose eggs (people sent them eggs from all over the U.S. because geese are hard to hatch), and they spent their honeymoon and vacations canoeing and camping on the North Shore of Lake Superior.

Back at his office, I asked John if people felt they were

happier in the beginning of the century, and he said, "From about 1900 to 1914, people were under the misbelief that things were all set now, that science was going to take care of everything. It was an atheistic age, I think. I see young people are now more inclined to belief than we were at that time. We put our trust in science. I don't know if it's betrayed us but it certainly has not solved the questions that we thought it would. They're still there and worse." The way John didn't believe in God intrigued me. It wasn't a lack of belief, as if he had a deficit; the urge to believe was simply not present in him, but he had a respect for people who, in his words, "have the gift of faith." John was relaying to me his niece's attempts to convert him to Christianity before it was "too late," when his wife Fay appeared like a vision at the door. I didn't know she was still alive. She had the slight frame of a dancer, with long white-grey hair and vivid blue eyes. She stood there until John urged her to join us.

Fay made John laugh and also drew him into sadness as she sat there withdrawn, due to cataracts, hearing and memory loss. With Fay next to us, John and I looked through black and white photographs he had taken in their early years: Fay painting on an easel along the rocks of Lake Superior, her hair blowing in the wind, with her high-laced leather boots; another of her sitting on a blanket with pots and pans strewn around her, the lake nearby, as she holds their first child; Fay in a beaver coat and stylish hat; and then ice skating, her leg curved behind her. A newspaper clipping showed her milking a goat, her hair shorter and more coiffed. In the photos Fay is jubilant, loving her life. We described them to her and I asked, "Do you remember, Fay?" She smiled, looked at me with her clear blue eyes, "Not really."

I drove the three hours home from Proctor playing mental Russian roulette: spin, cock, and shoot—the one left alone with the memories. Spin and repeat—the one who can't recall what she lived and lost. Years later the image that endures is of them holding hands. Both days they sat for a few moments with John's knobby fingers, mottled blue and brown like the rocks and cliffs in his landscapes, covering her slender pale hands. Time-before and time-after fell away and they were together, as they had been for seventy years.

Gone now, they are.

Leif wanders off into the brushy willow wetland adjacent to our backyard, on the other side of the path. Later he emerges and shouts, "I found a pond!" I can toss a ball from my screen porch to where he is standing. The girls and I work our way through the willows and thorny brush and stare at the secret pond, which is about the size of our living room. We put a stick down to measure how deep it is. The pond would have dried up before I discovered it, and now the kids catch tadpoles in summer and slide across it in winter.

I was pregnant with Audrey when I got a job working with seniors in Cambridge, and I was asked to start a group to help them write about their memories. Each week the women eyed my belly and marked the progress. A few days before my due date, Helma, who was in her late seventies, pointed her finger at me and said, "Pack your suitcase. One hundred percent make your automobile to be ready and prepare your husband." Then Helma read her story about the first day on the boat crossing to Ellis Island. Her piece was handwritten in German, and she translated it as she read about the 1200 Europeans thrown together on a navy military boat, speaking different languages, the men and women separated. Her little girl fell from the hammock three times that night. Other babies fell and she picked them up in the dark.

Marion followed with a piece about tuberculosis in her family. Marion was a regal woman in her seventies, and she was wearing pearls and high heels. From the time she was three, she and her brothers had to walk around the backyard every day for the fresh air, in order to fight off TB. In the winter her father plowed a circle in the snow, and they walked. At one point Marion broke into her story and told us about when she and her husband were on vacation in Duluth, and a woman came up to her on the street and asked if she was a Wahleen. (Marion was born and had lived in Cambridge all her life.) The stranger said she had dated Marion's brother, and it broke her heart when he died of TB at twenty-six. Marion looked at us and said, "That woman told me things about my brother and family that helped to make me who I am today." Her chin quavered and she went back to reading.

I walked down to the Rum River at the end of that day, and stared at the water while I made room for the women's stories inside of me. It was getting crowded in there and I wondered if the baby was coming that night. I fell into the enchantment of light on water and conceived of a myth about how babies are made: they are knit together in the womb with the stories they hear, and when they are full of stories and ready to make their own, they come into the world. A flurry of robins burst from the red berry tree on the edge of the woods, lifting and spreading out over the blue sky. Milkweeds had spilled open, the light shining through silky pods. Fargo the black lab emerged out of the Rum, shaking off water while Sadie the beagle sniffed the world of the river on her sleek dark body.

I had spent the afternoon cleaning our two-car-garage-turned living space, and I was complaining to Jeff as he marinated the steak. "The pink sink has that long crack where you dropped your razor. I can't get rid of the mold-smell in the entryway since the flood. And no matter how hard I scrub the plywood floors they still look dirty—what were we thinking of painting them Sunflower Yellow? After two years they look like Baby-Shit Green. And the cupboards!" (Which we had bought used— they came out of a dental office). "They are just so aggressively teal." Jeff shakes his head 'no,' like he does about ten times a day, (I hope he never gets Parkinson's because that would be his permanent gesture). I was a little on edge because our new friends, neighbor farmer Ken and his wife Helen, were coming over for dinner. Ken had jokingly referred to us as a Hippie Commune, and while I respect the hippies I've met, I wanted him to know we weren't what he might imagine that to mean— partner-swapping, pot-growing long-hairs who lived in a garage and let their kids run wild.

Dinner went well and we moved outside and sipped iced tea in lawn chairs on the patch of grass in front of our place. The kids were playing with the hose behind the barn. At the sound of shrieking we looked up as Cedar, Audrey, and Olivia came running around the corner toward us covered in mud—mud clotting their hair, covering their faces, and long streaks of mud down their arms and stomachs and legs.

I caught the glint of Ken's white teeth as he threw back his head and laughed and said, "Why they're buck naked!"

I met Fran Blacklock when I was on residency in Moose Lake to work on my novel at the Blacklock Sanctuary, which she and her son founded. She was ninety at the time. When I arrived at the cabin where I would be staying for two weeks, Fran was there to welcome me with a small glass jar full of kerosene. At the end of my stay the jar was full of wood ticks.

Fran is coauthor of *Our Minnesota*, and wife of the late photographer Les Blacklock. A few years later, when I asked Fran if I could interview her, I think she assumed my interest was mainly in her ability to tell stories about Les's life. While I admire his photographs and legacy,

I was taken with this woman who during the forties, walked away from urban life in Minneapolis and married a man who didn't have a steady job and liked to take pictures. Who honeymooned in a canoe in the Boundary Waters in late October. Who spent a summer in a nine by nine army tent on Isle Royale, a remote island in Lake Superior. Who lived in a fireshack in Moose Lake, and for a while made Christmas wreaths to sell from pine boughs they dragged in from the woods. And who, in her later life, could have subdivided and developed her forested acreage but instead chose to let artists work there and herons carry on nesting in their rookery. Like artist John Peyton, Fran's gleaming intellect combined with compassion brings to mind the ancient Greek word *to kalon*, whose meaning held that the good is the beautiful—the esthetic and the good (moral) were a unitary concept. I asked Fran if she and Les knew John Peyton, and she recalled his name and his paintings but had never met him. I like to imagine Fran and Les in their red canoe paddling past John and Fay in their silver one somewhere on deep and vast Lake Kichi-gami.

Audrey was about three, and her cousin Cedar, six, was over for a sleepover. We were lying in bed and I switched off the lamp. Audrey asked, "What's a lamp?" I was half-asleep and mumbled it was something that lights up. Cedar said, "So is the world a lamp?" My eyes flew open.

Some old people I would not hurry to catch up with on life's conveyor belt. They might have that medicinal odor that catapults me back to being ten and getting talked into visiting my friend Beth's grandparents on our walk home from school. When Beth opened their door the smell crawled up my nose and clung to me the rest of the afternoon. Or I might encounter one of many older people who have codified social norms so they exude an aura of shame and ought that drains the energy out of my body. But then there's Hudson, who during one of our many conversations handed me a cluster bomb.

A bomblet, actually. It looked like a planet, this metal ball that fit neatly in the palm of my hand. Part of my mind seized onto its sinister beauty: a perfectly round sphere made up of steel balls melded together with lead alloy. The bomblet looked medieval, like something you'd find hanging off the end of a chain. Another part of me was imagining the person that created it, how one could get caught up in its efficient and pleasing design. The rest of me was shot through with fear that the bomb was about to go off in my hand. (I knew Hudson was a pacifist, but still.)

Hudson pulled the two halves apart. "Normally there is an extremely high explosive wrapped around this small timer. At a certain altitude the timer goes off, which sends steel balls and lead shrapnel flying. Hundreds of these bomblets are released in each canister. They used cluster bombs on the Serbs. Some of the bomblets land armed and ready to go off, but not detonated." He waved his hand. "They're still out there."

My conversations with Hudson roamed from theories of black holes to whether there is violence in the nature of God. I interviewed Hudson because his experience of World War II felt to me like a missing story in our country's narrative about "the good war." Hudson was one of thousands of men who refused to fight for ethical and philosophical reasons, and was assigned to alternative service. The impact of Hudson's decision reverberated through his life, (including losing his teaching position, death threats, tapped phones, appearing before a White House subcommittee, and serving in non-combat with no benefits or recognition), and yet he seemed to hold no bitterness or contempt. When I showed up at his house to interview him, his wife requested that their names not be used, and that this never be discussed in the community in which they live. The U.S. military had recently invaded Iraq and patriotism was being drummed up to code red. It was both confirming and sobering to me when Hudson and his wife said they felt more afraid under President Bush's rule then any previous administration they had lived through, in spite of all that they had endured. The history of World War II is like a thousand piece puzzle; I survey the nine hundred interlocking pieces which reveal a panorama of the stories of the brave men and women who fought in the war, and my eye catches on the spaces remaining for the pieces that reveal the experience of Hudson and men like him.

"Grandpa Don is in that tree," Franny, five, said as we lay in bed with the lights off. She was thanking God for her loved ones and said this when she got to Jeff and Brett's dad, who had died just before Franny was born. From the kitchen window we can see the pine tree which was planted in memory of Don. When we drive by it, Franny says that he's in the tree, and though she doesn't seem troubled by this notion I figured I should dislodge the image of Grandpa Don curled up in the pine boughs.

"He's not really in that tree; his body was cremated, turned to ashes, which are buried under the tree in the ground. His spirit is somewhere else." I lay in the dark, feeling that I had opened my mouth only to replace one dark vision for another.

"What is spirit?"

"Um, the life force; what animates us, gives us life. What do you think spirit is?"

Quiet. "I think spirit is the thing that helps us remember the person that died, like how he laughed, and walked. The person wants us to remember and spirit is what helps us remember."

While I absorb the idea behind her words, I hold Franny's warm body and think about how some people die and they are gone, while others stay with us after their parting. I kiss her head and breathe her in and pray that I will never be far from Franny's scent.

We had been living on the land about three years when *Utne Reader* magazine accepted my idea to write an article about living with friends and building a straw bale house. The editor called to say she was sending up Judy Olausen to take our picture. I had heard Olausen interviewed on NPR, and liked her book of photography, *Mother*, with the cover photo of her mother on all fours on the living room carpet serving as the legs of the glass coffee table which was on her back. The day Judy was coming to the farm, I paced in our garage-studio, trying to talk myself down off the Ledge of Fear. Diane and I were the only ones home. She called from the farmhouse, "You wanna cigarette?" Neither of us smoked, really. We stood in her backyard next to the stump of the cottonwood that Allen the tree cutter had taken down a few years ago, and she rolled a fat minnow-shaped cigarette. The tobacco tasted like it had been shoved in a coat pocket since Halloween of '91, and the paper was wet with her saliva, but it was the body of Christ to me. I smoked it and lived. It brought me back to myself.

Judy arrived and I served soup and bread to her and my neighbors. She had us wear blue shirts and stand by the square bales in the barn, which were leftovers from Jim and Debbie's wall-raising. The only hitch was Debbie was stuck in traffic on her way home from St. Paul. The kids were restless, and Judy was anxious about the light changing as evening came on; she kept looking in her shutter mounted on the tripod. Taking the photo without Deb would have kind of punctured the concept. When she pulled up I handed her the blue shirt, and while her son Miles clamored for her she adjusted the neckline, and we found our places on the bales and smiled as Sadie and Fargo ran in and out of the picture.

When Cedar and Miles were in the second grade, their teacher asked me to visit the class to talk about writing because the students were creating and illustrating their own books. Though I was teaching in college, I was scared of being in front of a class of eight-year-olds. What if they thought I was boring? What can they grasp? And this was Milaca; only a few people there knew I wrote. I felt outed and fearful. Fear has been with me all my life like a crow cawing in my ear, digging its claws into my shoulder to secure a more permanent hold. When I can't make it go away, I can sometimes use it to my advantage until it lifts its wings and troubles someone else. Besides, it was Miles and Cedar in the class, with their brains glowing like neon.

With a pair of googley eye glasses and snakes popping out of a can, we talked about good writing. (Later the kids took the can to the back of the room and popped the snakes over and over.) Together we created a story about Brownie the rabbit and Po-Po the raccoon coming up from the woods along the Rum River to spy on our farm. It was Po-Po's idea, that rascally raccoon, to sneak into the farmhouse and climb on the kitchen table and sample Diane's blueberry pie. Brownie tried to talk him out of it, but she couldn't resist, and they left blue juice tracks on the white carpet. Since that visit I've returned often, and it's a comfort to be with the kids. They are themselves and don't yet know how or why not to be.

I was nursing Audrey and living in the garage when I was preparing for a phone interview with writer Anne Lamott. While I pumped milk and got up for night time feedings I was rereading Lamott's books, and remembering how funny she is. When I read her book in bed I giggled out loud and made Jeff stir in his sleep. Her humor doesn't undercut her depth. Sober after years of drug and alcohol use, and having suffered through the deaths of her father and best friend, she is in touch with that raw level of pain and grief that we all face at some point in our lives.

Here I was, in our renovated two-car garage home, staring out at the mud and spots of snow, waiting to talk with a writer who's book, *Traveling Mercies*, was a New York Times Bestseller. Lamott was on a tour and would be calling from a hotel in Ann Arbor at one thirty. An hour before the interview, I walked over to Debbie's house and dropped off baby Audrey with a bottle of milk. At one thirty I was sitting by the phone with six pens, a sheaf of paper, and a tape recorder. Quarter to two: Maybe she was late from another interview. I washed some dishes. Two o'clock: I wasn't going to eat anything in case it made my voice sound phlegmy, but I munched on crackers and an orange. Two thirty: I called the publicist in New York. "Just hang out. Anne's exhausted and might be sleeping." Three o'clock: In Anne's words, "the jungle drums started beating," and I imagined the arch of Audrey's back and her pinched red face.

Debbie sent Miles, four, down the gravel lane—the first time he'd walked it alone (with permission). I went out to meet him, and he was standing stiffly as the three giant dogs trotted up to greet him. He looked at me with his big blue eyes. "Your baby's crying cause she wants your milk." I gave him a bottle of formula. Three thirty: I thrust a Hershey bar into a jar of peanut butter and devoured it as I stared out at the sunny day, thinking, I don't care if she is Indira Gandhi, she shouldn't just blow me off. By four o'clock I was beyond anger and nerves. When the phone rang at four thirty, I expected it to be my husband. I said hello, dully.

"I'm so sorry. I slept through the scheduled time because I was awake most of the night. This is probably a terrible time to call." She sounded like she just got up. I imagined Anne with her blond dreadlocks in a t-shirt and sweats, with sleep in her eyes. Her apologies and all of that waiting leveled her out for me and we were free to talk about writing, raising children, having faith, and being women in the world.

I discovered I was pregnant the night before I was to fly out to Grand Rapids to interview Anne Lamott in front of an audience for Calvin College's Festival of Faith and Writing. In the midst of trying to pour shampoo and creme rinse into small bottles while holding Audrey who was one and a half, I mentioned to Jeff that I was late, and he got out a pregnancy test. It read a faint negative and I felt a mixture of relief and disappointment. Twenty minutes later I heard Jeff's voice, unusually small and quiet, coming from the bathroom where I left the test— uh, Linda.

How fitting to interview Anne Lamott on April Fool's day in front of five thousand people, at sea in that particular mix of hormones that seems to be required of me to make another human. Lamott's characters can be neurotic, angry, and petty, but they are also big-hearted and loveable. She allows us to laugh at them, which helps me to view my own coiled self with more humor and generosity.

Twenty minutes before we were to go on stage I waited for her in a back room. Though I had interviewed Anne over the phone, I was still nervous to talk with her face to face. She has the compressed energy of a mountain lion, or my mother—mysterious, powerful, you never know what she'll say next. You want to avoid bringing out the claws. Minutes before we were to go on, Anne wandered in and said "Hi." She sat down and rummaged through her large black canvas bag, while she was describing this obnoxious journalist who called her at her hotel and badgered her for a few minutes of her time. I watched her hands move through loose bills, pens, scraps of paper. "Hey look, Junior Mints—want some?" She asked the Calvin student and me. She knocked out two for the student, two for me, found one for herself and I held my breath as she searched for another one in the purse, digging down to the bottom. "Whew, found one," she said. "Like communion. Wouldn't be quite fair if you two got two and I got one. Anyway, I tried to explain to this guy that I was spending time with one of my best friends, that we were going to take a walk, and he said, 'No problem, I could rollerblade alongside you and ask you a few quick questions.'" We rolled our eyes. Her hands kept moving, finding the mirror, touching her blonde dreads, applying pink lipstick. "Oh, here's Sam." She showed me a recent picture of her son, stick thin, with a shy sweet smile, and I handed her a photo of my daughter.

As we stood up so the Calvin student could put on our microphones, Anne looked me in the eyes and said, "We can't fail. We'll do just fine. Can we pray before we go out?" And then we were holding hands with the student and Anne was praying for clarity and calm, for speaking what we believe is true, and asking the Lord that if someone was hurting in the audience, our words might give them hope. I have not joined hands and prayed with people outside my family since college days. And I needed it. The interview went well in the sense that I managed to ask Anne a few good questions that yielded long and interesting responses. Mostly I felt like Ed McMahan, sitting up there and laughing at the funny, startling things that came out of her mouth.

I picked up the phone mostly to stop the ringing and because I wanted a distraction from my writing even if it was only to hang up on what my kids call a 'money-stealer.'

"Hi. I'm calling from COAF and we're doing a survey. Question number one: If you were shopping today would you be interested in purchasing clothes or sporting goods?" I recognized Cedar's scratchy ten-year-old voice and walked out the front door to see her on her porch with the phone to her ear.

"COAF?"

"Cedar, Olivia, Audrey, and Franny."

"Oh, why sporting goods I think."

"Question two. Does a cold glass of lemonade and a brownie sound like a refreshing treat?"

I squinted to see the pitcher on the table, and Audrey, Franny and Olivia hauling stuff out of Brett and Diane's house. Noted the white sheets on the porch displaying sale items. "Why it suddenly does."

"Well for a limited time you can buy sporting goods while you enjoy a treat. Our sale hours are from ten to twelve. Have a great day!"

I put some change in my pocket and wandered over. The red bandana would look good on Audrey and Franny would like this book on stars. Jim must have received a call too as he was there shuffling through CDs. Brett emerged from the house and said, "Cedar, why are you selling Leif's baseball mitt? And those bird books aren't for sale either."

I keep waiting for my copy of Coleman Bark's translation of Rumi to show up at one of Cedar's sales so I can buy it back. Jim held up a hammer and looked at Brett. "Hey, isn't this the one I let you borrow a few weeks ago?"

It is the beginning of summer and I am in my office

downstairs trying to reenter the world of my novel, which I hadn't touched for the past nine months while I was teaching. I imagine this is like opening the garage door and encountering your 1959 VW Van engine that you decided to rebuild last year under the influence of too many beers. The smell of dirty oil assaults you as you step on a bottle top, and you bend over to pick up your diagram which you had scribbled on a stained envelope, and you recall thinking that you'll remember where all the parts go as you enjoyed the experience of pulling each one out.

There's a knock on my office door and I leap up in relief, and it is Audrey and neighbor Louis. Louis could be Audrey's little brother with his brown eyes and tan skin. "Can we use the shovel? We wanna dig for worms." I start to explain where to find the shovel then figure it's easier to show them. "Can we have a jar with a lid?" Soon my hands are moving through the cool dark soil in my garden and I'm gazing at worms and thinking about the wonder of them in our lives, how they can be both slick and prickly, what they do for our flowers and vegetables, and then I notice the state of my flower beds, and start pulling weeds. Franny emerges in the driveway from one of the neighbors' and follows me into the house for a pair of scissors, then outside again. As I am culling the wilted yellow lilacs, she asks, "Why are you cutting off a slice of heaven?" Diane and Cyndy drift over from their gardens, and we talk, then one of them mentions coffee and the possibility of some banana bread, and an hour or so later I return to my desk.

Multiply this experience by ten years. I remember telling a writer about our intentional cul-de-sac and she said, "You won't get the novel done unless you leave community." One of the harder things to reconcile here is working on larger writing projects and my insatiable desire to be in the thick of things. With fourteen other people nearby the possibilities proliferate and expand exponentially.

I had a summer cold; my throat hurt, I had a fever, and my body ached. Secretly I thought it was something more malevolent, though a few of my neighbors recently had the same symptoms. I was lying in bed on a bright warm day gazing out my window at the shimmery grass, the wind moving the leaves of the trees. The breeze was sticky, then gave me a chill. The grouse calling from the brush sounded especially hoarse. My dad was recovering from surgery too many states away, and I felt both very young and very old. I entertained the idea of staying in bed for the rest of my days— some combination of a physical malady and simply giving in.

I remembered an old friend telling me about how his father would do that off and on for as long as a month. His dad's pals would get wind of it and spread the word, "Oh, Heinie's back in bed." They'd drag in a few chairs and bring him beer. My friend recalled the sound of their voices, low and droning, punctuated with loud laughter.

Jeff could bring me my meals. As it is he usually makes them, and all he'd have to do is arrange the food on our wooden tray we keep above the refrigerator, once he shoved off all the kids' art projects I stash in there, which drives him crazy. I lie there, envisioning how the girls would come home from school and crawl into bed and tell me about their days and we would read books together. With this extra time I could actually learn how to French braid, and when they go to prom—suddenly Miles, ten, and Leif, eight, appear at my bedroom door with a Styrofoam cooler, sweat glistening on their faces, their blue eyes shiny, and their arms and legs tan and dirty. "Wanna see our frogs?" Leif asks. How boldly they approach the leprous crone. They both hold up a frog, careful to drip the duckweed and pond water into the cooler. "There's ten of them," Leif says, sporting a new gold hoop in his ear. "Wanna touch it?" Leif thrusts his closer. I stare at the Leopard frog's pulsing throat, the brown spots like cocoa beans against the emerald green.

"What's that?" Leif points the frog at my vaporizer. "Are you sick?" Perhaps they hadn't noticed I was lying in bed. Miles says, "We caught a garter snake too. You could come see it once you feel better." I find myself putting on shoes and swatting mosquitoes as I wind through the brush to the secret pond, back to the land of the living.

Inherited Beauty

(2006)

"What are you thinking about mom?" my seven-year-old Audrey asks while she and little Franny and I eat burritos at the kitchen table. "Aunt Rae's tea cups." We turn and look at the hutch displaying sixteen different cups from all over the world. "I drink coffee, I didn't want to collect china, but now that they were given to me I love them and serve tea to my friends. It's got me thinking about when someone gives you something you might not like right away, or don't see as beautiful, but because they gave it to you it changes your idea about that thing. Can you think of an example?"

Audrey chews and stares ahead. With her permanent front teeth and dark skin from the Romanian and Italian sides, she brings to mind a beaver. "Franny," she says. "I was jealous and she was chubby, but then she grew up and got beautifuller and her hair is as long as mine and she's fun to play with and now I like her." I look at Franny protectively. At five her face is mostly cheeks and blue eyes from the Swedish side. Franny climbs off the chair and goes to their bedroom, and when I move to follow her she returns with her photo album flipped to a picture of when she was a baby. She and Audrey sit on the couch and giggle as they name their relatives and friends.

For ten years we've lived in this intentional cul-de-sac with three other families, and I've become aware of how much my notion of what is beautiful is gathered from others. Neighbor Cyndy prunes and mists her house plants and they glisten, and her backyard gardens form a little Galapagos. We may be planting the same kinds of vegetables and flowers, but Cyndy makes them grow like they're from another planet. Years ago she gave me a cutting of her begonia and that plant has become the mother of many cuttings. Even though I've hacked it back like it was kudzu, it is person-sized and blooms lustrous pink flowers, and when you come into my house it extends its arms out to you like another member of our family.

Sometimes a gesture can be beautiful. In a meeting with my neighbors, I learn from watching one absorb a hard word without lobbing it back like a grenade. I think, next time I'm going to try that, I'll wait past my defensiveness and receive what someone says. That gesture is like a plant cutting: it generates life beyond itself. An action can be beautiful too. Last winter my next door neighbor and brother-in-law Brett leveled the ground by the garden, laid out sheets of white plastic lining that farmers use to cover their bales, bordered it in black plastic edging, and filled it up with water from the hose. Voilà—a skating rink—where there was snow between our houses there is a rectangle of pale blue ice. As I wash dishes I look out the window and watch my neighbors gliding around. My girls go from not owning skates to burying pucks. Beautiful, none of my doing, didn't even know I wanted it.

As I get older I see my familial inheritance as a kind of beauty in all of its chaotic complexity, because it is my portion, what was given to me. Memories are the mainstay of my inheritance. The soft, papery rolls of flesh on the upper arms of my Italian grandmother Adeline. We were surprised when she let us make them jiggle. The gold high-heeled slippers she wore around the house, her fingers dusted with flour as she pinched thumb-sized pieces of dough into gnocci (we called it covatil), which we ate with her red sauce. And by her blue Lazy Boy, Grandma's rosary and prayers she used every morning, noon and evening.

Audrey and Franny have few reminders of their

Italian and Romanian heritage. The hardest result of choosing to live in Minnesota among friends is how far away my family is. Around here the Scandinavian influence is pervasive and Jeff's relative are near (next door even), so the girls are growing up with Yulekaka and blue Dala horses, but you have to travel far to find a Romanian. What I experienced while growing up is remote. In the myriad of selves that make up my being, this self has no reflection in my day-to-day living. Living next to friends, not family, sharpens the edges around my childhood as being singular, unrepeatable, mine. As I watch Audrey and Franny sitting on the couch looking at the pictures, I remember when I was close to their age, staring at photographs a world away from here.

It is Saturday, Easter weekend, 1970. We pull into the gravel drive where Grandma Sophia is waiting for us in the backyard, with her hair in a net and her stout body in a faded cotton apron that hangs down to her black tennis shoes. She holds me in her fleshy arms. Grandma's voice is hidden, her words wrapped in Romanian like cotton swabbing; the way she says "cheekin" (chicken), "cinculation" (circulation). I look down at her hands—fingers like sausages, red-skinned, with dark man-nails.

Hands that packed meat for twenty years in the cooler at Sugardale factory, tended her half-acre garden, raised six kids, and fended off blows from a husband when he drank too much. Hands that made pigs in the blanket, mumaliga, ciorba, sweet flaky colac.

Dad and my two brothers and sister and I go through the back door of Grandma's little house and up the wooden stairs where Tusa Annie is waiting in the kitchen (Tusa [tusha] means "Aunt" in Romanian). Where does she live? Did she take the bus out here? Years ago, steam from the ancient roller at the laundromat where she worked shot up in her face, and I am careful to look in her one good eye. Her black hair is singed and she tucks her hand in her pocket to hide the nubs where her fingers used to be. Annie has a way of making herself smaller than her four and a half feet. It is easy to forget she is in the room. I wonder if that saved her now and then, growing up. As I got older I would make a point of talking to her. Her voice was low and hidden and the hard part was realizing that she was sane.

The creak of the steps announces arrivals. Tusa Mary comes in with a cake in a plastic tub from the Echo factory where she works. "Hi honey," she says in her raspy voice. "Commere and give Tusa a hug." There's lipstick on her lit cigarette and she has the same bulldog chin as her mother and sister Annie. My Dad's relatives have dark hair, skin, and eyes, and I have red hair and freckles like my mom, who is Italian and plays Chopin on a Baby Grand and says words like "plebian" and has a dining room set and crystal in hutches and mirrors on the wall. I have no memory of being at Grandma Sophia's with my mother.

Cousins Greg and Jeff come in and when I hug Dawnell I have to press in to keep from slipping off her nylon jacket and four-hundred pound body. She has caramel skin and thick glasses and a cringing smile. "Hi Linda Jo." Retarded is a word they use to describe my cousin Dawnell, like you'd say short or quiet, and it carries about as much weight. She seems alright to me. Dawnell says things that make me laugh and think. I remember the time Dad talked Grandma into going out to dinner because he wanted to give her a break from cooking. Grandma crinkled her nose but finally relented if we went to "the Co-la-nel" because they have "good cheekin." When we got to the Kentucky Fried Chicken, Dawnell couldn't fit into the seats or the booths. "I've tried it before in KFC," Dawnell whispered to me, and then hung her head at the watching strangers, the flurry from the manager coming over with a chair from the back, which didn't work either. We ended up at Bob Evans. Dawnell and Grandma liked the biscuits and honey.

Grandma limps over to the mantel and brings down the mason jar. I stare at the jagged gray stone in her hand as she tells me how she was mowing the lawn by the mailbox when the stone shot through the mower and lodged into her leg. Her face crumples at the memory. After yelling for help she dragged herself to the house where she called one of her daughters. I sit on the couch in the living room cramped with relatives, and my eyes move from the black and white photos on the wall (close-up of Grandpa George who died before I was born, with his buzz cut and Hitler mustache, staring out at no one), to the mason jar on the mantel. The stone looks like all the others in the driveway, yet it is set apart. Later I will think about how Grandma is comforted by holding the stone, by being able to locate the source of her pain. So much pain has lost the memory of its origin.

Aunt Helen pauses at the top of the stairs to wave at everyone before she puts her food in the kitchen. She has dark brown hair and eyes and a slender body like my mother's. She lights up the room with her warm smile and hugs. Tusa Helen writes me letters through the year, and when I go to her house she feeds me ice cream sandwiches and fixes up a pole with a hunk of Velveeta cheese on the hook so I can fish the creek. Tusa Helen is everybody's favorite, in part because they almost lost her. She is the youngest and when she was little the family was so poor they were going to have to give her up. They couldn't take care of six kids on a barber's salary and what grandma brought in. The kids begged to keep Helen, and my Dad and his brothers were farmed out to relatives and neighbors to work for their boarding until ends could meet. Dad remembers sleeping in an attic space just big enough for a dusty old bed. The winter wind blew through gaps in the chinking and the rats scurried along the rafters. Aunt Helen's our favorite because she loves each of us like she doesn't lose sight of the fact that she is here because of love.

Thud-thud. Slow heavy steps. Uncle Gordon fills the narrow door frame, hand cocked on his gun holster, waiting until all attention is on him before he claims the room. My eyes dart from the thick red scar on his cheek to the photograph of Helen and Gordon at their wedding: she is in a flowing white gown and gloves, looking over her shoulder, he is in his Navy uniform and spit-shine shoes, also staring at no one.

We squeeze in around the dining room table covered with a cleaned and ironed cotton cloth. It seems there is so much to eat that all the food can't come out at once. We dunk Grandma's soft crusty Romanian bread in our supa de gaina (chicken soup), trying to scoop up some of the slippery thin noodles. I am aware of the creak of the floor as my tusas and Grandma go in and out of the kitchen, and of the fear of being noticed by Uncle Gordon, but mostly I am caught up in eating slice after slice of Grandma's bread soaked with broth. In her calm voice Tusa Helen keeps the conversation going with questions about school and our mom and her stories about working in the dental office. Grandma brings out sarmale (stuffed cabbage) and slices of mamaliga, cooked corn meal that Dad had stirred earlier with a broomstick in a metal pail. Far into the meal I sense before I notice that Grandma has stopped her path from the kitchen to the dining room and has finally sat down on the chair nearest the door. From the look on her face she's thinking about the next thing needing to be done. Dad and my tusas bring her into the conversation and for a brief while she eats with us. She lets Mary and Helen serve their desserts and then we settle into the living room.

"C'mere Red," Gordon says after a few beers, his hands folded over his belly. "Sing for me." I freeze; Aunt Helen nods sympathetically. I am told when I was four I would climb on the table and sing "Sixteen Tons" and "The Cotton Ball song" ("When I was a little bitty baby"), but now I have crossed over. When does it happen for other girls? I am the elephant man, distorted, goony, aware of my limbs and lurid hair and big nose and caved in chest and longing only to be unseen. "Sing for me Red." I shake my head no, but his look and pat of the thigh form a command. Later, I will think, *Is this when it begins?* Moving past all self-will to please the man across the room?

At the end of the song Dad rescues me with his ukulele. I escape to the kitchen and find Tusa Mary smoking at the table, looking out the back window at the trailer, the garage and the dump beyond. I go to the sink for a cup of water and from that window all I can see is Ashland oil refinery—dirty metallic buildings and pipes taking up a city block—and rising above the buildings is the lone metal stack with the giant orange flare. I squint to see the thin ladder leading to the top of the stack. When we drive the four hours to Canton we know we are close to Grandma's when we see the eternal flame and Dad says, "After high school my job was to keep that going." I sit in the back seat and feel wonder at Dad for being the keeper of the fire. All the farms around Grandma's house are now owned by the refinery, and every time someone from Ashland shows up at Grandma's door she shakes her head and says no. They are waiting for her to die so they can buy it cheap, because who would want to live out here now? I sip the water and it tastes like the refinery looks.

Mary beams at me, "How's school honey? You look just like Tusa Helen." She grabs me in her arms, sits me on her lap. "What are you learning? Johnny's so proud of you. Your Dad's a prince, you know that? He's the best one of us, besides Helen of course."

We watch out the window as Denny parks his truck in the grass and gets out with his Rottweiler on a short leash. Denny, my Dad's cousin, is a god to me. Ripply black hair, shining eyes, a smile that cracks open creating dimples, and muscles under a white t-shirt and jeans. What I like is Denny doesn't seem to know he's handsome, or if he does, he understands it doesn't count for much. Dad comes out the back door and they stand in the grass. A shadow flickers across Denny's face then passes as he throws back his head and laughs. Dad has a bond with Denny because Denny's father was kind to Dad when he was growing up, something his own father didn't know much how to do. One time Dad and Denny were out hunting in the woods behind the house and they found a human skull.

Denny loves Dad, but even more he adores my grandma. Tusa Mary and I watch as Grandma hugs him in the backyard. Denny's talking too fast and all worked up and my Grandma walks with him while she gathers branches from a recent storm and puts them in the burn barrel. She mostly listens, and from the kitchen window I can see his shoulders relax, the tightness in his face smooth out, and soon he's letting the dog loose to sniff around. Denny won't come in the house so we go out to see him.

I stay behind Dad while I take in his beauty and shyness, praying he won't notice me and hoping he will. Soon he is calling for the dog and we wave at his truck banging down the long gravel drive.

Upstairs at Grandma's the rooms are cold and full of secrets. Dad and my brothers and sister stay up there. Dawnell and I sleep in the living room in the hideabed of the ancient couch, smelling of dust and bottoms. Dawnell's side sags. At first it is fun as she tells me stories about her school, how she lets the boys kiss her and likes it, and her Dad coming to visit her (he's married to another woman with a family in Pennsylvania; never got around to divorcing Tusa Mary), and then it happens like all the other sleepovers. Dawnell jerks up, stares wide-eyed out the window, "What was that?" "What?" "There, look," pointing to something in the lurching darkness, her eyes bulging behind bottle glasses. "No, what?" She's panting, moaning and whimpering and then we both start screaming for my dad, Dad, *Dad, Dad*! Though I know he'll be mad I am comforted by the squeak of the stairs, his puffy eyes, mussed hair, and white t-shirt. "What's all this shouting?"

"Dawnell saw someone out there," I cry. Dawnell's covering her face and bawling.

"There's no one out there." He turns the porch light on, takes the broom and swats out the door. "You girls stop tellin scary stories and get to sleep." Lights out, Dawnell turns away, her body a mound next to me, like she's disgusted with me or something. I lie awake in the dark trying to make sense of things.

Easter Sunday morning I find Grandma stirring farina over her white gas stove, pouring sugar, and salt, and cracking in an egg so that it gives the cereal a warm yellow sheen. We put on our good clothes and go to the Romanian Catholic Church. It is strange to see Grandma without an apron and in a dark heavy dress and black dome hat with a net, talking with other short ladies I don't know. If I am lucky I get to sit on the end of the pew and kick my leg out and watch the priest move slowly up the aisle, spraying us with wet smelly incense that makes my nose itch. I stare down at the prayer book, words like scratches, look up at the man in gold with his back to us like he's performing some magic trick. We can watch if we like. The trick takes forever to set up, lights and gold and swishing of robes and Latin and Romanian — *bucci bucci bolli* — the women behind and above me in the choir sing in their loud high voices. There is nothing pretty or familiar about their music but they are on my side of the church, they are real, and they are women. I listen for the *bucci bucci bolli* and *a-men* and know that these parts of the mass are for me. Finally the priest turns and holds up the magic golden cup for us to admire. It is finished. Some collective tension or suspense is released and we are spilling into the aisles, going up to tear off a hunk of bread (no flat wafer like at our church at home, but bread that someone made), and sipping the sharp vinegar wine that makes my eyes sting. We move from person to person offering bits of our bread, *Christos a inviat*, "Christ is risen" and receiving it, *Adevarat a inviat*, "He is risen, indeed." The church echoes with the murmurs of people offering each other the body and blood of Christ. I look in the filmy eyes of old people, the bright eager eyes of boys and girls, and they gaze on me in love and me with them, and we are one, and it seems like my whole life I am trying to get back to that good feeling.

Down the dark popping wood steps for sweet nutbread culac and coffee, and here in the church's belly the ladies are comfortable and in command. On the drive back to Grandma's, Dad and I stop at his cousin Jake's and we stand in the kitchen, Jake with his Tasmanian devil red hair and raspy voice more air than sound, pouring Dad hooch in a shot glass, which they toss back. Dad sways a little and wipes his eyes with the back of his hand, and Jake laughs, and then they sip the beer, me off to the side watching them. Jake notices me all of a sudden, his wheezing chest rising up and down, and he says, "You remind me of Nutsie," (Aunt Helen's nickname).

A flower blooms in my chest; a crown is placed on my head.

At Grandma's we sit down to more food and bowls of colored eggs—the prettiest eggs I've ever seen. Blue and purple marbled with veins of green, red and orange, and what do we do with them? We tap each other's egg and if ours breaks we must eat it. All of that cracked beauty.

Gone now, they are. Like lights blinking out on a dark hillside. Aunt Annie's shrinking ability worked too well. She was walking across a parking lot and the truck driver never saw her in his rearview mirror. This was before it was required for trucks to have back-up signals. Whenever I hear the beeping of a truck I think *Tusa Annie!* A kind of prayer in reverse.

Denny got married and had a child, but the darkness that hovers over this family and takes hold of some more than others gripped him in a way that made his wife afraid for him to be with his kid, and at thirty Denny took a gun and shot himself. (An uncle went the same way.) Like Grandma Sophia's stone, I can trace my desire for a certain kind of man back to Denny. The Italian janitor's son under a full moon on the golf course in Yellow Springs. The long-haired native construction worker in

Ashland; while we sat in his truck I kept an eye on his totem bag dangling from the rearview mirror. Walking in the glistening rain in Urbana with JT, my fingers catching on his black curls. I felt alive in their laughter and wildness and darkness, and lost in the excess of drinking, smoking and failure—their failure to stay open and my failure to understand that love wasn't a cure.

Tusa Mary got fired from her line job at Echo two years before retirement and had to move into her mother-in-law's little house with Dawnell and her son who is divorced and has the sleeping disease, so sometimes he falls asleep while he's delivering pizza. They watched roller derby, smoked filterless, and Mary changed her mother-in-law's diapers and turned her in bed and tended her till death. Because of the accident, even though Grandma preferred Helen, it was Mary who took care of Grandma and sat with her in the nursing home. Tusa Mary ended up there too. I called her a few months before she died and she said, "All I want is a cigarette, honey. Bury me with a carton of generics and I'll be happy. I'm ready to go."

Gordon and Helen were driving down the highway when two boys went left of center. Gordon turned the wheel toward them and they plowed into Helen's side. A few weeks after Helen's funeral, Gordon showed up at Grandma's in a new truck he bought with the settlement money. Helen was the closest thing we had to a saint, the best person alive, everyone agreed. Later, when I learn to deconstruct, to no longer believe in people as good, I will criticize her for staying with Gordon, but I came to understand that even that can be seen as a kind of good.

All deaths are not equal. All losses are not the same. When Helen was killed it fundamentally changed us. She was our consolation. Sure the family had bad luck at times, but you don't realize that you feel the world or God owes you until someone vital is taken away. Grandma's limp got worse, as did her memory. A few years after college I came to Canton with my dad and it turned out to be the last visit I had with Grandma Sophia. We were sitting at the kitchen table. She was squinting to look out the window at the dark form of my dad moving in and out of the garage, barn and smokehouse that, many years earlier, she and her husband George had made out of cast-off railroad ties. (The dark spot in Grandma's eye is where the nail that she was pounding into a tie for the smokehouse ricocheted up and pricked her.) The backyard used to have a coop where Grandma would catch chickens by the leg with a hook she formed by bending a clothes hanger. Dad remembers chickens hopping around the yard after he'd chop their heads off. Grandma Sophia also kept a horse, a cow for milking, and pigs they'd slaughter. She would grind up meat for sausages and use the intestines for casings. Dad remembers chicken claws in the soup, and the time George slaughtered his pet goat. Dad refused to eat it, went hungry that night. "That was my pet," he said.

Grandma rubbed her palm over her eyes and peered out the window, "Whozzat," in her soft, high voice.

"That's Johnny, your son. My dad." She looks at me surprised. "Johnny? When did he come? You got a boyfriend?"

"Joe. He likes to fish."

She sighs, shakes her head, "Don't ever get married." She and George didn't know each other in the old country though the villages they grew up in were only a few miles apart. When she came over at fourteen the marriage had been decided upon. Grandma picks up her salt shaker, the glass kind with a dented aluminum top. She's had the same one all these years. When Dad found out she had diabetes he bought her a new shaker that didn't pour out so much salt, but she refused it, so Dad snuck a piece of scotch tape under the old metal lid to cover some of the holes. I can see salt granules stuck on the tape. "The baby," Grandma says, "she came out so small, and she couldn't suck, couldn't hold on. Oh I tried and tried, we boiled rice and tried to feed her the milk, nothing." The pain on Grandma's face like it was yesterday.

When I ask Dad about it, he remembers then that there was a baby between him and Helen. A hard birth at home; she couldn't latch on and lived only a few days. Grandma buried four of her seven children.

I feel like I was asleep, or under a spell while I was with them, and then I was busy living my life in other places with other people. When I awoke to the inheritance given me they were gone. So I live on memories. When I moved to the country and put in a garden I remembered Grandma Sophia tying up her beans and tomatoes with panty hose. I planted apple trees and recalled sunlight flashing on aluminum pie pans she hung in her cherry trees to scare away the birds. I birthed my children in the hospital with Jeff by me, and I pictured Sophia in her narrow bed with the midwife, and George and her kids waiting in the hall. When I'm tired after a long day teaching I see Tusa Mary on the factory line, Annie leaning over a wet pile of someone else's clothes, and Grandma walking in the predawn to the bus and hiding her pregnancies on the meat packing line so as not to get fired. Conjuring up my relatives doesn't lesson my load but turns me toward gratitude. They keep me company in my living.

Grandma, how did you dye those lovely eggs? You burned trash in the rusted barrel out back, but where did you burn your bitterness and disappointment and anger? Faced with such darkness, how were you able to have faith, to keep on loving?

Sophia, Annie, Helen, Mary, George, Gordon, Jake, Denny, baby. Here, I give them to you. Their bodies have gone to ash and when you come up the aisle I thumb their ashes on your forehead and they mingle with your skin, singe your middle eye, and become one with you. They look out from inside you now, but don't feel their lives as tragedies.

At my Dad's third wedding I danced with little kids and old ladies who were somehow related to me, and Great Uncle Ted Sima with his blue eyes and white head of hair that was level with my nose. Uncle Ted was usually the one who started the dancing at the family reunions in Timken park that we went to while I was growing up. The food streaming out of the cars seemed endless. I chased cousins around in the grass while women put plates and bowls on picnic tables. Later, as the light settled on the cotton tablecloths, Uncle Ted pulled Grandma Sophia from the cluster of women and she laughed and resisted and then for a moment I saw her body could do more than cook and brood over the next meal. Dad and Uncle Charlie got out the broomsticks

and helped each other remember the traditional dances they learned in the Romanian classes they had to go
to after public school. They moved those sticks around
their bodies and jumped and were slim and lithe as Fred
Astaire, and everyone was leaning in, singing, clapping,
and remembering the source of their belonging.

My house was closing in so I walked down to the Rum
River and watched the wind kick up. The trees creaked
and moaned and threw back their arms like my relatives
at a reunion. The river flashed mercury then rust, and I
thought about the blood that runs through Audrey's and
Franny's veins. Mine, yet not mine.

My grandparents formed communities through a
shared culture in order to survive in a new country. My
neighbors and I live alongside each other mostly due to
friendship. I want to stir my ancestors from their sleep
and after I've cleared up a few things—"Tusa, do you still
think the Lord gave you that giant goiter on your neck?
Would you have gotten it removed so you wouldn't
have to spend the last ten years of your life sleeping in
a chair?"—I would ask them what they think of my life
here and note the ones who shake their heads in refusal,
and lean toward the ones who recognize what we hold in

common—kinship.

Our is a different kind of kinship that, early on, led Audrey and Franny to ask questions like, "Why is Auntie Leah not Louis's auntie?" and "Why does Cedar" (their cousin) "come to Grandma Lou's for Thanksgiving but not Olivia?" (their neighbor). After parsing out what is familial, and what is the farm, they accepted it with the ease that belongs to children. Audrey and Franny have lived with these people on this particular piece of land all of their lives. The Rum River, the meadows, our neighbors and friends, are also part of their beautiful inheritance.

It's invisible, what is most different between my daughters' lives and mine at their age. What is hardwired in me and absent in them is the feeling of waiting for the other shoe to drop. The shoe of fear that's the size of the truck that killed Tusa Annie. Audrey and Franny are scared of the dark and might worry from time to time about us leaving them, but there are no lone shoes in the closet of their psyches. Yet.

I do not live in imminent threat of a hostile new country, of being beaten by my husband, or of having to face giving up a child. But at times I feel like an old calliope, one of those steam-powered keyboard instruments found on riverboats and circuses that make whistling musical sounds. Different calliopists control my melodies, but the ten-year-old who is me blows a shrill whistle of alarm while holding a shoe and peering anxiously at the sky. She is sounding the call for the moment when this intricate balance of peace, borne of hard work and grace, will be snatched away.

Soren Kierkegaard's book, *Fear and Trembling,* gave words for what the ten-year-old sees—the guillotine over each of us. Like Abraham's knife raised over Isaac, I saw the blade poised over my relatives as I was growing up, and now I see it glimmer over my daughters. The flash of it is revealed in moments like when Franny walked out of the ice cream shop the same second the girl barrelled down the sidewalk on her bike, so that when I looked out the open door I heard the screech of the brakes and saw the wheel bump Franny as she stood there holding her cone. Wheels are everywhere. Franny will die, as will Audrey, and me, and you. I only hope that angels exist, and that there is one whose sole purpose is to sit and feel for what we lose every day.

Enough about blades now, unless they're made from wood. As I make my way up from the river I see Audrey and neighbor Louis climbing on the tractor, swinging swords and spears made from culls from Dana's woodpile and lashed with masking tape. Audrey and Louis have roped a blue sled to their bike to haul their arsenal around the compound. And over by the garden,

Franny and Olivia are walking along with pink fairy wings strapped to their backs, holding stuffed animals decorated with jewelry that sparkle in the sun. They are deep in their imaginary worlds, as am I, and I think, is this a dreamland my friends and I have created where we can play out our dreams? Where we are free to see what dark, startling, mundane, and joyful stuff our dreams are made of? Ah, then let us play them out a while longer.

Buddha in the Compost

(1996-1997)

The kitchen smells of too-ripe-too-full-nobody-wants-to-deal-with compost. I open the cupboard door under the sink, swat away fruit flies and push aside the white plastic lid perched on corn cobs, tomatoes, coffee grounds, and egg shells. After topping it off with refried beans, I lug the pail out by the garden to the bin which was here when we all bought the farm. It is a square of chicken wire nailed to two by fours, and I see that the dogs have tunneled their way under, which explains why our beagle Sadie is releasing gas bombs in our bed at night. A grasshopper whacks me on my cheek as I struggle with the latch. My own compost is smelly enough, but add six other humans'. The food scraps include their saliva, their smell, their very essence commingled with red sauce, bread crusts and guacamole. When I dump the pail the stench whooshes up into my nose and clings to me like the slop that splashes onto my leg, and in my aurally altered state I see in the compost the face of Buddha. It doesn't look like Jesus or even Che, it is female, and I'm not Buddhist, though I read a lot of writing by people who are, and I often feel like I have a Zen double that pops up in my life, like when I feel the need to control things or defend myself, or when I can't sleep (usually due to defending myself to the invisible other), and as my mouth opens and out comes the ways I'm not what I feel accused of, there's a part of me occupied with what the Zen version of me would say; what would she do? Sometimes she helps me take a deep breath, but mostly, like the compost-mirage, she vanishes. The mosquitoes have discovered me, and as I head back to the farmhouse I think about the vision of the feminine Buddha. She looks like the statues and pictures I've seen, and her playful smile and serene countenance seemed to be reflecting back my choices. You want to live in community? Here, taste and see.

Eight years ago, when my friend Debbie and I starting dreaming about buying land together with friends, we were sharing a cabin and studying theology with a community of professors and their families in a renovated logging mill in the Oregon Cascades. While we were on the mountain we heard about how some of the

communes tucked further back in the woods were de-
volving. Friends who had bought property together in
the seventies were dividing up the land and moving on,
away from each other. Their endings were somehow a
backdrop for our beginning as Debbie and I talked about
building our houses and raising kids alongside each
other. Through the years our dream of living together
was like a donkey we prodded along the road that we
sometimes shared and sometimes didn't. Some of our
good friends longed for the same thing and seven of us
borrowed money from banks and family and purchased
this farm and acreage by the Rum River. Over the past
year we have been extricating ourselves from jobs and
leases and moving onto the land. My husband Jeff and I
got here a month ago.

   Back at the farmhouse I scrub the white pail with hot
sudsy water, pondering how it is that plastic molecules
seem to have a tribal memory for every smell that's ever
settled in them? The improbability of us coming together makes the venture all the more entrancing, but deal-
ing with compost causes me to ruminate on challenges,
like space. We can't retreat to our own caves because we
don't have any. For the first two weeks Jeff and I lived in
a camper parked alongside our VW Van, then we settled
into a small bedroom of the farmhouse we are sharing with Debbie, her husband Jim and their one-year-

old Miles. Our friend Dana's sleeping in the apartment he's building above the garage and joining us for meals. When Jeff's brother Brett and his wife Diane and their daughter Cedar visit from International Falls on weekends, there are seven adults and two kids sharing one small bathroom. The toilet seat wiggles, and if I move a certain way the whole toilet shifts and I find myself staring down at brown wax from the ring that clearly, no one is supposed to see. Some don't flush pee, others gag at the sight and smell of it. Some want both lids up, others leave them down. This one buys recycled toilet paper, another prefers Charmin. Bits of hair cover the sink, bras and underwear hang from the shower rack, toys float in the bath, and wet towels are draped everywhere.

The nub of a universal truth is exposed in our lives here: we need each other in order to make it. We're working on building Jim and Debbie's timber-frame straw bale house first so they can move out of the farmhouse in time for Brett and Diane to move in next summer. Dana will need help renovating the garage and barn into a home, and Jeff and I have to figure out temporary shelter until we have the money to build our place. Dana and Jim are timber framers by trade, but they haven't built with straw bales before, and the rest of us are inexperienced laborers. In the past I have cleaned toilets, picked zucchini, waited tables, balanced books, and recently completed an M.A. in literature, but none of this work included framing walls and post and beam construction. It's humbling to learn as we go.

Dinner dishes are cleared, and Jeff, Dana, and Brett head back to the house site. The foundation is poured and they've put up the joists and the cap over the basement. As Diane puts Cedar in the backpack and I look for my camera, I am thinking about how we chose the building sites. Last winter when Jeff and I were still living in Cincinnati, we drove up for a visit and trudged through knee deep snow with Jim and Debbie to stand at the edge of one of the hayfields. We looked out over our fifty acres, and considered the river's floodplain, the sun's exposure, the views of meadows and trees, and the neighbor's black and white Holsteins. I tried to beam in the spirit of Per Hansa, the Norwegian pioneer in *Giants in the Earth*, but not the ghost of his wife Beret, who eventually goes mad on the prairie. I remember being struck by how wonderfully ridiculous this freedom was—to choose where to one day build my home, to be able to live in this beautiful place with these good friends. Mostly I felt like we were children playing house in the fields of the lords.

As the sun sets, Diane and Cedar and I walk over to the barn to take pictures of the hundred year-old Minnesota white pine timbers, planed to long smooth rectangles. We head through the meadow to the site and snap photos of Brett, Dana, Jeff, and Jim working in the basement; of Fargo the black lab, Georgia the German shepherd, and Sadie running through the tall grasses, and Diane's two horses in the meadow flicking off flies.

It was like a slight of hand, the way fall swept in. Yesterday it was warm and full of summer light, and today the sky is flinty blue with clouds moving fast, the horses are prancing in the field, and the trees are making that shirring sound. While the others work on the house, Debbie and I lug the trash barrels into Brett's 1962 pale green Dodge pickup and drive the five miles to Milaca. I like watching Debbie behind the wheel, with her jean jacket and blonde hair. At four feet ten inches her feet barely reach the pedals. The pickup spits and bucks and the bottles roll around as Miles sits between us in his car seat with the tip of his finger in his mouth, his blue eyes taking it all in. The guy at the recycling center checks every bottle and tells us to wash them next time. I gag on the smell of the brown liquid mixed with butts. As Debbie pulls out to Main Street, the truck stalls twice then sputters as she drives over the curb into the gas station where it bucks forward and dies. An old man in overalls watches us and chuckles, saying, "We're having some fun now, eh."

Back at the farmhouse I marinate pork chops, put potatoes and pumpkin pie in the oven, slice the round sunflower bread and go out to fire up the grill. As I'm dumping in the black chalky bricks I realize I've never started coals before. There was always a man around. I squirt them with fluid and light it. Nothing. Read the tin can, push the bricks into a volcano shape, squirt more and start weak flames here and there. I holler for Debbie and she douses the coals with half the can and the flames leap high. Earlier Debbie had walked through the meadows and picked a fall bouquet of reddened sumac, Black-eyed Susans, goldenrod and purple clover. The red wine in her orange and blue glasses made by a local blower looks and tastes like fall.

The frame of Jim and Debbie's house is up. The yellow pine timbers look like a dinosaur skeleton against the blue sky. While Dana and Jeff and Jim screw in sheets of plywood for the floor, I cut rebar poles with the electric saw. The poles will be placed in wet cement then we'll impale the straw bales on the rebar. There is a satisfaction in measuring the pole, pulling down the blade and making a clean cut. I feel like Rosie the Riveter as sparks fly to the scream of metal burning through metal. I could do this all day; I could cut enough rebar for the world! But after awhile my arms hurt and my ears ring and I trade the saw for a screw gun. Then Jeff and I quit for the day and walk the loop of trail through a meadow of milkweed, clover, and purple thistle. We round the bend to the Rum River, the sun sparkling off eddies, the sound of water taking its time yet getting there. The Dakotas called it Spirit River, or River of Good Spirits, and the whites interpreted "spirits" as alcohol, hence rum.

Jeff lathers on Dr. Bronner's Peppermint soap and bathes while watching me staring at the river. He tells me about the way he feels around the other guys at times, and I am protective of the little brother part of him. The malaise grows and I want to leave—go back to Cincinnati, to a movie, or to storage to get our TV. We walk through the woods of elm, maple, and oak dotted with swampy ponds. Stinging Nettle and mosquitoes drive us out through the meadow leading to the teepee Brett and Diane put up earlier this summer. The scarlet sumac is a red rash behind the stark white canvas. Brett and Diane tried to stay there on their visits but the mosquitoes, heat, and no water drove them into the farmhouse. I pull back the flap and find it is wet still; toys, clothes, and dishes float around. Brett and Diane remind me of nomads with their ability to leave everything and move on. The place looks like they stepped out to go for a walk, only there's standing water, and they haven't lived in it for a month.

We have a clear-blue sunny day for the wall-raising of Jim and Debbie's house. Friends come up from Minneapolis and St. Paul and help us load the bales from the horse shed into Brett's old Dodge. The oat straw bales are from the neighbor's field adjacent to our land. At the site some hoist the bales up to others who impale them onto threaded rebar poles; the tight rows remind me of giant shish kebabs. I look around at our friends, the sweat making straw cling to everyone's faces, hair, arms, then up at the house taking shape before our eyes, and I have this rare feeling that we are part of bringing something good and useful and beautiful into the world. In one day we bale all of the walls. Then we hike through the woods and swim in the river and let the water carry away the chaff. Back at the farmhouse we eat and drink and watch the video Brett is making of building the straw house, then rewind it and watch it again to laugh at ourselves.

At six in the morning, I stumble out of bed and knock on the door of the little room in the farmhouse we've made into an office and find Debbie standing in the dark reading her sermon. She and two friends started a new church in St. Paul and it's her turn to preach. I go back to bed and after Jeff's alarm goes off for the third time, I find her in the bathroom, scribbling on her draft. What a humbling job to be a minister; to try to speak the word of God and navigate your own will like a boat-motor propelling you into deeper waters. Her text is in John, and she is writing about how we really don't love each other well, but when God says to love one another it is a command, an imperative. "Abide in me." Live as if you are reconciled to each other, as if you are loved, because this is so. It is not up to us to figure out how to love perfectly, as if the command is a high jump; it is a given, now live as if it is so. Talking with Debbie about her sermons makes me feel like all of life's whittling down might be for some good purpose.

A lot of the work on Jim and Debbie's place now is stuffing straw into the gaps between the bales. The house is the Scarecrow in Oz and I am padding him into life, or in this case helping Jim, Deb, and Miles stay warm. It's a bracing thought that I can affect the number of drafts in their lives. The bales are then covered with chicken wire, which will be stuccoed over. I like how Dana and

Jim make things up as they go. When they come to a problem, like how to adhere the bales to the timbers, they read the *The Strawbale House* book, puzzle through the situation together, and then wing it. I sit on the floor and cut electric fencing wire into strips to make hooks that will pin the chicken wire to the bales. I hand the wire to Jim's dad who threads them through the bale to Jim's mom, waiting on the other side of the wall. I hear her muffled voice, "No, can't find it, try again, wait its way over here." I hear Jeff holler as he scrapes his knuckles again on the nasty metal lath above the door frames. Music's playing, sun is shining, and we are building a house no wolf can blow down.

It's cold and there's no heat in the farmhouse. The repairman who jimmy-rigged the oil furnace said it's been on its last leg for ten years. My unhappiness wears me out. We have taken on an adult-size task here. There is too much to do always. An irony that we move to the country to simplify and end up driving for hours and working ourselves like farmers. But then Miles sees me and his face lights up as he says, "*Lin*-da." And when Cedar's here she puts her arms around me and looks at me with her blue eyes and little apple-shaped face and says, "Linda-*da*." My computer's making gurgling sounds and the printer churns out faint text with a white line through it. I am writing a grant to interview an old writer/artist up in Duluth. Debbie's in the office working on a sermon, Diane's in the living room writing her Masters thesis on the red-eyed vireo, and I'm in our bedroom struggling to achieve an alchemy of words that will convince someone to give me some money.

The roof is up on the straw bale house. Giant blue and brown tarps covering the bale walls bring to mind a Christo art piece. Jim lies awake in the farmhouse at night worrying about the bales getting wet, as mold would spread and rot the straw and the wall would have to be torn down and rebuilt. In the morning he stares out the kitchen window, searching for signs of rain.

This weekend is the big push to get the house ready for stuccoing. As I type I hear a semi full of gravel crawling down our drive. The dogs bark incessantly at the tractors, bobcats, and trucks. Steve, an old friend of ours, came up for the weekend to help. In 1983 Steve and I went to the Oregon Extension, the college program in the renovated logging mill nestled on the Greensprings in the Cascade Range, where the professors and their families live year round and students share cabins for the semester. Four of us from the farm went to the Oregon Extension. Saturday night we all sat around talking about what "home" means. Steve said so many friends he knows our age don't live where they think will be their home. Our choice to live together, to buy this property, has shifted things around, made people think. In that moment I realized I need others to affirm what we're doing here. Debbie agreed. It's like a marriage; you want people to encourage you. I was thinking about people's projections about the community at the Oregon Extension. Already I see it in the visitors who come here. They imagine something more idyllic, planned out, lots of time sitting around talking and laughing and drinking until we fall into bed. We have those times, but they're haikus interspersed by long verses of day-to-day living. It's still good and worth it, but like marriage, other than our dreams.

Sunday comes and we are straining to get the house ready. Jeff's working the bobcat to fill in the water ditch. Dana's in the six foot trench bareback with a chisel, digging a hole through clay, sweat on his back and bald head so he looks like a prisoner. I take Miles to St. Cloud to pick up Jim and Debbie's front door at Menard's. Dana's red beater car has no exhaust, dented sides, and a broken window, but it's got a sturdy rack. During the thirty mile drive Miles falls asleep with a finger curled in his blonde hair and another in his mouth. I wake him in Menard's parking lot, and he clings to me and I feel strong with him in my arms, protecting him from the overlit aisles full of people and things, my red hair flowing out of a black headband, wearing my garage-sale orange and blue wool jacket and stained sweats and hiking boots.

We walk to the millworks area where a kid drives around in a cart searching for the Larson door; he comes up with three but none are Jim's. Eventually they find it and when the guy puts it on the rack I hand him Dana's yellow nylon ropes, resisting the impulse to explain that none of this is mine—car, door, baby, ropes, driver's license. When I jump on the fender I notice a dent and scratches on the new door. The guy undoes it, finds another, cinches that on, then we're driving home.

Back at the farm Debbie's gone to church and everyone is still working on the house. The afternoon drags on and I'm mad at Jeff because I want him to take over with childcare or at least to tell me what a great job I'm doing. My capacity for needing praise is endless. When he comes in I haul the recycling to the garage, throw the compost in the bin (no Buddha today), burn the paper trash, then go upstairs and cry as I strip off my clothes and take a shower, feeling like I'm going to get some kind of cancer from working so much to meet everybody's needs. I get out of the bathroom and pass Jim in the hall and he thanks me profusely. It's hard to feel sorry long when I think of Debbie going to church to be a pastor after working on the house all day, and Jim rushing around to get himself and Miles ready to drive an hour and a half to St. Paul so they can look at childcare places. No time for them to sit and feel relief, to drink a beer with us and savor the fact that they did it, we did it, we got the house ready for stuccoing. Dana and Jeff and I wave from the porch as Jim drives by, Dana in his Carhartt pants and army green Milaca Building Center cap.

Tonight there is a chance of frost. I end up with an afternoon alone and walk down to the river, taking in the clear blue sky, the scent of autumn, and the coolness on my skin. In the woods I find the remains of a struggle—blue-grey feathers with white tips, a coil of worms and two green claws. Sadie sniffs each one. Emerging from the woods I walk past Jim and Debbie's house covered in tarps, nod to the horses, and when I get back to the farmhouse I realize that I've never seen a key for the house, never known it to be locked.

At dinner Debbie told us about when she was pulling out of our driveway and saw two trucks parked at the road. She braked to say hello to the men peering into our property. One of them asked, "So how many families are living there now?" She mumbled two, when there are really three, and drove on. Yesterday a small semi brought in eight loads of sand for Jim and Debbie's septic. Each time the driver passed by he'd crane his neck around looking at our green VW van, the two other foreign cars, and Dana and I working in the garage. The other day Jeff got pulled over a half mile from our place by a patrol for no apparent reason except he didn't have tags on the front plate, but more likely for his long hair and out of state plates. People in town at the bank, grocery store, and library, politely want to know why and how we ended up in Milaca. When Debbie and I dumped the recycling, the guy heard us discussing in terms of "we" and asked us if we're with a group. I said two families had bought property together and imagined him mentioning it to his wife who works at the bank, who mentions it to her friend over coffee, whose husband issues permits for building. Meanwhile, Jeff and Dana and I are converting the garage into two illegal living spaces, and after the farmhouse it's the first building you see when you drive in.

The stucco men back up their truck to the barn, filling their barrels with the hose. It's the first time they've worked on straw. The warm breeze and sunny day draws me out and I wander over and take pictures of them applying the grey cement-like stucco with trowels, the straw still exposed below them. I head back to the farmhouse and am writing from the second floor office, and spying on Ed the septic guy who is putting in a mound between the straw house and the garage space we're renovating into our living quarters. Ed has a big ruddy face, barrel chest, and works quietly and efficiently. Sadie is barking and I get up to see the horses moving toward the house from the lower pasture. I stare as in a dream as they amble over to the garage. Tula pokes her nose at the tools, snorts, rears back and they skitter off. She and the grey gelding Whinny head to the house, tossing their heads. I call their names, wave carrots and lead them to the stables. I wrap some wire around the gap in the fence leading to the septic mound. Ed mentioned the bees were bad; they stung him and the horses seemed jittery down at the meadow.

Jeff, Dana, and I make black bean and rice burritos in the farmhouse and talk about our expectations for community. We discuss how haphazard our choices seem; seat of the pants, individually made, how we'd like to have had more planning about where the houses go, the possibility of a shared well and septic, if we are indeed a community or merely neighbors. Before we moved here I expected spontaneous gatherings where we'd read

Mary Oliver or Wendell Berry and crank up Captain Beefheart and paint murals on the walls while discussing solar power and God, but the hand of necessity has been slapping us forward. Jim and Debbie need a house right away, we need shelter in time for Brett and Diane to move down in July, and there's hesitancy on everybody's part to pull us in any direction.

It's cold and dark early now, and everyone's weary of working on the house. Winter draws us inward and the cold reminds Jeff and me that we need our own place in a few months. Jim goes out before light to the house and returns for dinner. My unemployment ran out and I'm working at the garment mill in Milaca and the printing press in Princeton. When Jeff and I aren't working we are renovating the garage, and Dana ricochets between building sites. In my mind, and maybe in others, I thought we would all work on Jim and Debbie's house until it was done, then when the next one was ready to be built we'd all pitch in on that. Necessity and human limitations had other ideas, which makes me rethink my notion of community for the hundredth time.

I edit a book on birds as Jeff mends the fences so the horses can graze in the meadow. Debbie calls out questions from her room as she works over the draft of her sermon on "Loving your neighbor as yourself." Plenty of fodder for this topic. Life here has thrust my humanness in my face; my selfishness, need to be liked, need to fix things. Jeff and I lie in bed and remember how easy life was in Cincinnati. Here our meals are spent with the others, as are our evenings, which is fun on one hand but leaves me with little patience for Jeff. I feel less present with him because I spread it out on the others. I don't know how not to. One despairing, grey day I drove around Milaca feeling like I was the exact wrong person to live in community, the emotional weathervane that I am, sensing turbulence, impending storms, I turn and turn and never get it right. Debbie's had similar moments. She ends up feeling like we try to appease her; she does want the house clean but she doesn't want to feel like an ogre because of it. We realized we all take turns feeling like the outcast: Dana because he's the one with the knowledge to build all our homes, so he works too hard and is placed in a leadership role, then feels resentful and uncomfortable; Jim has talked about feeling like the worst member of the community; Jeff feels incapable of being loving and around everybody so much; and Brett feels unabashedly selfish. Diane and I work overtime keeping others happy, which ends up backfiring. She told me that when I first came here she thought to herself, "Linda is being too nice," which meant she would have to be nicer to keep up with me.

Community life is like the Rumi story of a man asleep on the side of the road. A holy man on a donkey rides up and sees a snake crawling into the sleeping man's mouth. The holy man beats the man and forces him to eat rotten apples and makes him run until the man vomits, "the good and the bad, the apples and the snake." Life here brings out everything coiled inside each of us, springing out of our mouths. It's about time.

Diane and Brett are here for the weekend. We ride the horses to the river, Brett leading Winnie the gelding, with Debbie holding Cedar in the saddle. Jim pushes Miles in the stroller, Jeff and I follow along and at first Dana resists, saying he has so much wood to chop, then relents. When we walk across the lower meadow, Winnie balks at the layers of ice and the dogs tussling around her hooves. Brett eases Winnie past her fears. Everything and body looks beautiful in the blue winter light. The river is almost level with the banks; the layers of ice and snow shift our gaze to the dark flowing water on the other side of the island. Through the woods snow is falling off of trees, sparkling against the rough bark.

A few of us head back to disassemble the teepee. She is so simple to take apart. We gather the small twigs and sticks that hold the canvas to the poles and work the mosquito netting out of the frozen ground. Only the poplar poles are left standing, creating an airy triangle, the space still hallowed. Brett lifts the main pole, then decides to leave it up, and rests it back on the others in the wrong place. He shrugs and says, "It doesn't matter where it sits." I stand there mentally shifting the pole back among the others against the blue sky, when Jim steps forward and says, "I can't stand it," and gently lifts and rests the pole in its place.

Jim and I split wood while Dana works the chainsaw and Jeff stacks. It feels good to know we're helping Dana. Keeping things near even may not be the way of grace but it makes life more comfortable around here.

Sometimes I am aware that I'm an Italian-Romanian Catholic among Scandinavian and German Protestants. This leans on my feeling that I don't know how to live with people anymore. The rubber band of my self has stretched, then snapped back to its natural place, which is alone with Sadie and Jeff in a house, not one tiny room crammed with our bed, the odd angles of the ceiling stealing precious space. Last night Jeff and I moved things around, trying to come up with a configuration that would let him get to his clothes without bumping into the dresser. We sit and stare and end up putting it all back where it started, only now each of us has a little shelf for our important things.

And yet the light is so warm and clarifying, making me notice the grain on the old red barns, the severe slant of the triangle-shaped roofs, the deep brown coats of cows and horses, the bluish tint of snow on houses, mailboxes, and black-green pines. I linger in the barn and pet Sylvester's black fur. While I look into his green eyes I tell him he's a good barncat, and I feel him purr. I head back to the farmhouse, where Miles and I draw fish, me listening to him talk in sentences. Dana comes home from the store and gets stuck in the driveway where the snow drifts over the field. Miles and I watch out the window as he takes the big shovel off his rack and scoops methodically, then Jim goes out and gives him a push and soon Dana is making chili in the kitchen. Jim and Debbie eat bowls full before they head to St. Paul for church.

The other night we were talking by candlelight in the kitchen about life together, then we started in about the tractor. Tractor, tractor, tractor—the consuming focus for Dana, who never wants to be snowed in again. He wants us to buy a large used IH Farmall for six thousand dollars. We talked about how every piece of technology has its dark side, its potential to kill, and Dana is frustrated with our milquetoast responses to buying the tractor. Community life is like being married to six people, only we don't have sex and sleep together and wake up and hold each other and share the pockets of our day so we can mend. We must open our mouths and work it out.

A few days later I am driving home from the garment mill in Milaca, where it was sleeting, and just before our road it turns to big sloppy flakes of snow. I pull into wonderland, hear the roar of the tractor, and I sit on a strawbale and pet Sylvester as I watch Dana nudging forward a big round bale of hay with the bucket, the snow a mantle on his green wool coat and black beret. Sweet cherry red tractor.

We tapped the maples behind the farmhouse. Jim and Debbie tapped them last spring and showed us how to drill a hole and use hollowed out elderberry twigs for spiles. From my desk I look out at the plastic jugs hanging off the trunks, waiting for the sap to flow. Some have started already, others haven't heard spring's wakeup call yet.

A garage door is a hard thing to disassemble. Jeff and I are making slow progress. I try not to think about living my life over a sandpit where people have been dumping oil for who knows how long. We drive to the ReUse Center in Minneapolis for used fixtures. Dana is a little appalled at the old windows and doors, which are hard to put in, and will be drafty in the winter. If it were his choice they would be brand new and double-paned. We find a bathtub for twenty-five dollars and teal cabinets for the kitchen that used to be in a dental office. We put in large square sheets of plywood for the floor.

While we work we keep an eye on the sap boiling on the propane stove outside; the smell of the sap in the giant metal pot is faint and sweet, but when it's transferred into the kitchens for the final boiling down and canning, the odor becomes dank and cloying. We eat the dark sweet syrup on pancakes, oatmeal, waffles, and with our eggs even.

This early morning while driving home in the dark after the night shift at the printing press, I was pondering the reality of the possibility that these are the people I may spend my life with. As I pulled into our gravel drive, I rolled open the sunroof, the night and the Big Dipper framed in the space, the warm-cool air filling my car. The moon cast its glow on the farmhouse, the barn roof, and the cars. I turned the radio off and cut the lights to see the stars better and for the first time I heard the chorus of frogs rising from the marsh.

Jeff and I are moving up! From a camper to a farmhouse room to a garage. Friends come from Minneapolis and St. Paul to help all of us move in. We rent a U-haul van and Jeff and I drive to our storage space and fit our goods in one load, and then fill up both small rooms of our garage studio. We pull the van up to the farmhouse where friends are packing and marking boxes, and load and haul Jim and Debbie's goods to their new timber frame straw bale house. A sudden storm leaves the men over at the straw house, me in our new studio, and the other women in the farmhouse. I stare at the sunflower yellow floors, the white walls, and it feels delicious to be alone between houses full of people I love.

Summer light reveals the beauty around me. The Green John Deere tractor baling hay. Father and son hoisting square bales onto an open truck. The corn tall and shimmery in the bright July light—waving its silky arms like women welcoming their soldiers home. The green round bales dotting the lower meadow remind me of slumbering creatures caught in a moment of stillness.

The evening light settles on them like a blessing.

This morning I looked out my bedroom window in our garage studio, past the septic mound to see Jim and Jeff standing over a four hundred pound bathtub, trying to figure out how to get it up to the second floor of the straw bale house. Later I hear the pt-pt-pt of the red tractor and watch as they drag the hulking white beast into the bucket, maneuver it up to the balcony, then hoist it inside the door.

The shrill rattle of Sandhill Cranes beckons me to the front window, and as I watch a pair tunnel through the sky with their measured wingbeats and long straight necks, I see Dana and Cyndy walking down to the river. Light glints off her barrette and the piece of grass she has between her teeth. Cyndy went to Bethel College with Brett and Dana. I don't know who thought of her and Dana first: it crossed our minds, and theirs, and love bloomed before us. I pitied any woman Dana brought home, with six pair of eyes on her, but Cyndy fits in so well. The kids love her, and Dana is so happy.

Brett, Diane, and Cedar have settled in the farmhouse, Jeff and I and Dana and Cyndy are in the two levels of the garage, and Jim and Debbie and Miles are living in their straw bale house. Mostly it is a relief to have our own dwellings, but I am very aware of walls separating us. I miss the conversations at the table and in the hall. We shift from being with each other all the time to needing to plan dinners and meetings. The farmhouse and garage are as close as next door neighbors on a city block, and even though Jim and Debbie's house is a stone's throw away—just past the horse shed—it feels like they live in the suburbs. But we are in and out of each other's houses. The kids abandon their trikes and bigwheels and wander in, heading for the refrigerator. The dogs eat each other's food. I find our wooden spoon over at Diane's, Debbie's glass in my cupboard, my bowl at Cyndy's. We borrow eggs, coffee beans, toilet paper, tools, a car. The nice thing about community is you can always find a car.

I come out my back door and climb up the wood stairs to check on the puppy Dana brought home from work and Cyndy adopted. She is a small white mutt who got Parvo and has been fighting to live. When I open the door she slips out, wags her tail, and curls up next to me on the screen porch, the sun beating down on us. I shield my eyes to watch Jim and Miles's slow progress past the horse shed, and along the gravel driveway. Miles has on black and yellow rubber boots and the Cincinnati Reds baseball cap Jeff and I gave him when he was born. He is three now and it fits. When they walk up the stairs the puppy lets out one yip, and in that moment I think that she just may make it.

Dostoevsky on the Rum

(2004)

A commune, a planned neighborhood, an intentional cul-de-sac, the compound. What are we? For eight years now, four families have lived next to each other on a piece of land in rural Minnesota. Others have offered up these terms, which feel like logs tossed at the woodpile of meaning. "Hippie Hollow," the latest one, was dubbed by a friend and nearby farmer. I like the hippies I met in the Oregon mountains, but I am not one of them. We are middle-aged friends who bought land together and are living and raising our kids alongside each other. It continues to make good sense.

The men are from Minnesota, and the women either went to school in or visited Minnesota long enough to know we could live here. We wanted to live by water—a lake or a river—and forest, and be close enough to the

Twin Cities, but not too close. Seven of us had to agree, and the farm, with its farmhouse, barn and garage, meadows, and woods along the Rum River, was the first place that felt right to all of us. Now we are four couples and seven children and a few horses, cats, and dogs on close to a hundred acres. When we first moved here, I felt like I was a Romanian-Italian Dorothy landing in the Scandinavian Protestant farmland of Oz. Now I see that others before and after have been blown out here by a similar longing for a little land and some quiet, and by larger, invisible forces that connect city and country.

Our place is a few miles beyond Princeton whose welcome sign reads, "On the Growing Edge," and just shy of Milaca, a town of 2,500, where most residents have known each other's families for generations. Milacans don't look like most people walking down Grand Avenue in St. Paul. When I go to the library or grocery store I see tired women with large hands and strong bodies, and old Scandinavian farmers with faces that look like they're shaped out of silly putty; a pinch here for a mouth and there for watery blue eyes. When I first moved here, I thought people were unfriendly. It took me a while to realize they just don't think that a smile or conversation is an essential part of money changing hands.

Our property is surrounded by corn and soybean fields dotted by silos, old farmhouses, black and white

Holsteins, and faded red barns. We ski and hike our trails and fish and canoe in the wild and scenic Rum River. Over an hour away from Minneapolis, we are squarely in the country. Or so we felt. Now, like water brimming over, markers of change surround us: For Sale signs, modular homes, sub-developments along the river, old buildings moved onto land, and posters for farm auctions at the grocery store. Take for example the dairy farm next to ours, still owned by a member of one of the original Dutch families who settled here. One brother is still farming and the other subdivided his river frontage property and is selling it off piece by piece. We are witnessing, and to a certain extent a part of, a portion of the million or so acres of farmland and green space America's losing to development each year. (In the seven counties surrounding the Twin Cities, it is at a rate of sixty acres per day.) As people move from there to here, and the light rail gets closer, and a Caribou Coffee opens up a half hour away, the city feels like a big sweaty guy jogging too close with his wheezy breath and shiny warm-up.

Who's to blame for sprawl? Real estate people subdividing and selling to well-meaning folks who want a little peace and some nature to look out on? Burnt out farmers selling off the land for what they feel is rightfully theirs? The cities' lack of affordable housing that nudges people to move out here because land is cheaper? Overworked planning commissioners in rural counties—underpaid locals who either don't have the time to fashion a vision or aren't given the budget or legislative teeth to follow through with their good intentions? Agribusinesses that effectively devalue the price of meat, grain and milk and force farmers to get big or get out? The false price of gas that allows people to move out here under the illusion that they can afford the miles one must cover to find work? Capitalist values that harvest the vital organs of a community? Religions that continue to endorse the maxim to be fruitful and multiply? The colonial impulses seeded in our loins that propel us to move and acquire, move and acquire?

As I attempt to untangle the Gordian knot of what historian William Cronon calls the "self-destruction of the pastoral", the winds of change are howling in my ear, making a shirring sound in the skeletal remains of the corn rows. Down the county road there is a one room schoolhouse, white, weathered, with an annex added on. It is the last and only one of its kind in Bogus Brook Township. Though weary from a century of fighting gravity, it looked structurally sound when we moved here. Our insurance man owns it, lives across the road from it, and was in fact a student in the last first grade class to attend that school. When I asked him what his plans were for the building, he shrugged. "My wife wanted the oak flooring for our kitchen and friends are taking what they can use. It's a hazard. I've been meaning to tear it down, just haven't gotten around to it."

Impulsively I asked him if he'd consider selling it to be moved, either to make it the town hall by the Rum River, or perhaps our future home. Could he come up with a figure for what he'd want for it? He blinked, mouth parted. Later, when I told my husband about my idea, it turns out he had had the same instinct as he drove past the schoolhouse. But then we had another baby and the hurricane winds of life with two toddlers swept through our garage-turned-living space and left everything stirred up and in a state of chaos. Moving and restoring an old building was not an option. So it goes for most people. Immersed in our daily lives, we see the changes but it often doesn't go past looking out the car window and having a mental tug of war about protecting what is good and adjusting to the vicissitudes of sprawl.

A new family bought the farmhouse across the road and subdivided their front yard into four two-acre lots. A modular home springs up near our mailbox. I have never gone over to introduce myself. I am leery after what happened on the property next to them, which was owned by one of the original Dutch families, and has the tallest oldest white pines around. The place was bought by a "nice family from the suburbs who wanted to get away from it all." Within a year, the father had shot his neighbor in the leg for shooting their dog in front of his kids. He went to jail and his family moved back to the suburbs. The neighbor who mows and bales our hay has told us other bizarre stories of people who have moved in, and then on. It brings to mind William Cronon's comment that, "The act of fleeing the things we fear reproduces them in the landscape we're in."

I went to a Planning Commission meeting addressing a proposed subdivision on the Rum River just south of us. A few weeks earlier Jeff and I canoed the stretch of the river from Milaca to Princeton, and tried to identify the area the subdivision would be built. Turtles plopped off of logs, and an otter slipped in and out of the water. We paddled past forests of oak and ash and white pines, with an occasional farm peeking through. South of Milaca we rounded the bend to a house looming before us. From our canoe I could bounce a tennis ball off the side of it. We stared in silence as we floated by this conspicuous dwelling, the kind you'd find in a wealthy suburb. Soon the trees reclaimed the land, sun sparkled off of eddies, and we were caught up again in the fall splendor.

Back at the planning commission meeting, the property owners were a good looking couple, tanned and clean-cut, the kind you would see on a commercial for Grand Cherokee Jeeps. Their surveyor passed out maps displaying the five acre lots, the houses one hundred feet from the river, the cul-de-sac road through wetlands. When a committee member pointed out that the lots were in the floodplain the property owner shot back, "No they're not." When another member said the DNR has concerns about developing in the wetlands and floodplains the landowner replied, "'So and so' did it, I know we can." He was referring to the house we canoed by—the precedent setter. If this subdivision is approved, the next property owner will come before the Commission and say, "This couple did it, so can we." The domino effect along the Rum.

I left the meeting hoping that the DNR could stop them, but the DNR is only as strong as the acts it upholds. From what I can tell, the Wild & Scenic act doesn't keep landowners from developing away the wildness and scenery. And what good is a Wetlands act if people can find loopholes to build roads right through them? Money has patience and tenacity and power. Herons are silent, pull no weight in the world of property taxes and bottom line profits. Otters don't compute. Fish disappear without a sound.

How do you measure the value or convey the teeming life inside the ark of a tree, or a bog, or that mysterious bridge between water and land we call floodplain? Take the floodplain along the Rum River—full of smaller trees, messy branchy undergrowth—this indeterminate transition between water and land. Imprecise, changeable, and essential, it resembles our democratic process. Not much to look at in a glance, it can only be understood by staying put, year in and year out, and in the spring listening for the ice to break like the boom of a freight train, the river tossing chunks far beyond what one would think was floodplain. Then as the weather continues to warm up, waiting for the river to crest to see how far it will flood. It is much easier to fill it in, put a structure on it, and make it useful for pete's sake. Writer Jim Harrison said, "Nature answers her own questions and none of our own. The misery is created by asking the wrong ones."

It is a diverse assortment of people who live out here—farmers, laborers, commuters, retirees, factory workers, and teachers—but everyone can agree that we want to preserve the farming life and protect the natural beauty. We want to keep it country. I think even the handsome couple wouldn't want this place to end up looking like the retail section of Elk River, Minnesota. The bloated retail strip along Highway 169 reminds me of the photo of my fibroid tumors. As Harrison put it, "If you do not believe land can lose its soul, look at land that has lost it." Could this soullessness have anything to do with the fact that the Elk River area has had the highest number of suicides in the state? In just over a decade the population nearly doubled: rural families mixing it up with urban families like colliding tectonic plates. In the city of Elk River alone, there were eight suicides in four years: seven students, and a teacher who walked out of the classroom and onto the tracks of an oncoming train. The train, one of the first mechanical nodes of connecting city to country.

No longer do I see the city as this distinct entity or even a gestating beast that spawns little faux cities. The lines that connect go both ways. The corn, soybeans, dairy, and meat produced here go to the city to be processed, and then return to us via grocery stores and power lines. Some of the nitrates used on Minnesota cornfields filter into the groundwater, then flow into the Mississippi River, and end up contributing to the "Dead Zone" in the Gulf of Mexico. We could not live in the country, as Cronon points out, without oil, which comes to us via the city. He sums it up, "City and country are different aspects of the same system. One can't survive without the other."

A constellation of lines link us to each other, the farmers, the forests and river, and, what's become especially clear since the events surrounding 9/11 and the war in Iraq, to those across the globe. I imagine these lines forming a fishing net of coarse hemp, tended to by my Romanian grandmother, Sophia. Her hands were strong from working at the meat packing plant and coming home to cook for six hungry children and a husband who got mean when he drank too much. I see her bent over the net, fingering the lines, testing the knots with her rough hands.

Picture the furrow of Sophia's brow when she comes to the tangle that is sprawl. It seems to reflect the absence of a structure, but sprawl is actually shaped by overlapping systems that bundle up too close together. As she works to unravel this snarl, Sophia would discover that one of those lines is color-coated. There is no billboard out in the country stating "Whites Only" but look around, and white is mostly what we are. "Sprawl is the new face of Jim Crow" says john a. powell, executive director of Minnesota University Law School's Institute on Race and Poverty, in a *Minnesota Magazine* article by Micheal Finley. "Thanks to sprawl, powell asserts, America is more segregated than the day before the Supreme Court ruled on . . . Brown vs. the Board of Education in 1950." Through census maps and careful research of documents back to the twenties, powell and others at the institute revealed the systematic laws, zoning rules, and tacit assumptions that prevented people of color from moving out to suburbs and beyond. As he puts it, "The outward aspect of this movement seems at first glance like the natural result of free movement. But there is nothing natural about sprawl."

The insurance man stopped by the other day. I looked at his ruddy cheeks and imagined the line connecting him, a native from a farming family, sleeping and eating in his house, to that weathered schoolhouse outside his window. And the one linking me, who has a vision but little resources or contacts, to him and to the building, and I longed for a community that was and is not yet. Then I paid my insurance bill.

This net transects time and is flung back into our history, woven by democracy and capitalism, which are like the Odd Couple on that old TV show. Felix the capitalist is neat, efficient, and aware of the bottom line. Oscar, our man for democracy, is messy, smelly, takes his time, and doesn't seem to always have a method. As the nation gets increasingly inculturated into Felix's way of thinking, we are impatient with democracy's ponderous, incremental pace. So we vote in a rich Texan, an oil man who speaks in simple black and white terms that appeal to that part of us that wants a king.

We have less of a vision for such outgrowths of the democratic process like strategic planning for rural areas, community involvement in mapping out cities, and increased taxes to support education and affordable housing. We grow rusty in the way of real exchanges and start to feel like this kind of ongoing conversation about long term processes mucks things up and wastes our time and money. A citizen's committee to plan for green spaces is akin to Oscar's smelly sneakers blocking the hallway to the back door of unfettered development.

Felix, a believer in allowing the 'free' market to take care of things, would look askance at our life in the cul-de-sac. Fiscal nightmare—who owns what? Resale value? Adolescent dream—grow up! What kind of job can you get out there? Oscar would plop down on our couch and have a beer with us because he's not so trusting of the market; he sees society as a constellation of communities that are essentially related to each other, and that people thrive by participating within a number of those overlapping groups.

Which brings me to my moment of insight as I was driving into our property the other night. I was staring at the lights from the farmhouse, and our building which is home to two families, and the straw bale house beyond. A gravel thoroughfare connects us all. There are lawns and swing sets and gardens and a garage. And out here in all this open space I can hear my neighbor Cyndy cough and watch my brother-in-law Brett stare out the kitchen window as he washes dishes. It dawned on me that we had made ourselves into a little village.

Aside from producing a short bark of laughter, this thought prompted me to consider how we are doing by the standards I use to gage the health of a city. In terms of housing, we are using the existing buildings as homes for three of the four families. We mull over the impact the building materials will have on the region and the environment, and sometimes this affects our choices. The bales Jim and Debbie used for their straw bale house were grown in the field adjacent to ours, the timbers were harvested from a private wood lot in Minnesota, Jim and Dana did most of the building and the rest of the labor was subcontracted out locally. Soon my husband and I will be building our house. We've seen how far the river floods in a high water year—really really far—and we've experienced how the nearness of the houses affects daily interactions (the farthest home, though only one hundred fifty feet away from the others, feels like it's on the next city block). We're building on the highest yield hay field and it will take a good portion of it out of commission, so we can start cultivating the lower fields now.

We are protecting much of the land by clustering the houses far upland of the river and leaving the majority of the property communally owned and undeveloped. We have too much lawn which most of us mow with a polluting two-stroke tractor mower and push mower. A joint septic system for three families requires us to buy petroleum free soap and be aware of what goes down the drains. Some of our compost goes in our gardens, which yields some of the produce we eat in the summer. We buy what we can locally, otherwise must drive to get our food. And driving is where we really falter. We all own at least two cars and drive a lot. We share rides when we can, but it is not systematic.

In terms of quality of life, kids have it best here. Parenting alongside my friends has helped me to stay sane and made me a more accepting mother. Our children move freely from house to house and feel loved by eight adults and each other. They are learning early how to get along, from creating games that are fun for both seven- and three-year-olds, to what to do when there aren't enough swings to go around.

After years of living together, I'm no longer shocked at how poorly life in white middle class America prepared us for community living. Picture eight adults trying to decide where the wood-fired hot tub should go, or what color the playhouse should be painted, or whether the garden beds should be raised, to tougher decisions like how to divide up the land and what to do if one of us chooses to leave. (Now what do we call ourselves?) At times life together can be a psychic meatgrinder, and some days my husband and I feel like community is a hairshirt we want to shrug off so we can move to a house in the city where we walk to a get a good cup of fair trade coffee or eat a spicy Thai dish. Where we would get to know our neighbors if we want to, and allow them to see only our gregarious and kind selves rather than the judgmental, angry, threatened, and hurt people that we also are. Communicating is a freighted, complicated venture in trust. If it is hard for us, who love and know each other well, then how do we have a prayer for succeeding in the larger community?

What gives me hope is we have experienced each other at our worst and we still feel grateful to be neighbors. We are at times better at talking and listening to each other. Recently we purchased forty acres of adjacent land, and I was aware of how much more smoothly that process went. There's a kind of invisible, stuttering, process that is occurring with us as we learn to live with each other, on this particular, beautiful piece of land.

So when the river crests and reclaims what we consider our hayfields, or when the beavers chew away at what has become our forest sanctuary, I feel a little less ignorant. When spring rains flood the narrow gravel road that usually separates the neighbor's cornfield from a marsh full of frogs, turtles and redwings perched on cattails, and the soils and water commingle, and I imagine the fertilizer and herbicides mixing it up with the intricate music of the birth and growth cycle of those marsh creatures, I realize that the road, which seems like the sure hard thing, is one line of hemp. Crisp divisions—our property, their cornfield—are only a few strands in a much larger net. Our world is multilayered, above, below, and around us.

Maybe our former Senator was onto something when he told my neighbor/brother-in-law he should move to Russia. That was his retort when Brett recommended controlling development along the Rum River. We all should retreat to the Russian world of Fyodor Dostoevsky's novel, *The Brother's Karamozov*, published in 1880. In it he writes: "We are each responsible to all for all, it's only that men don't know this. If they knew it, the world would be a paradise at once. . . For all is like an ocean. . . a touch in one place sets up movement at the other end of the earth."

I think of Dostoevsky's words as I drive past the schoolhouse and the afternoon light shines through the holes where windows and siding used to be. The building looks like a drunk's mouth full of broken teeth. Along this county road there are faded barns at various stages of folding in on themselves: long slow exhalations, visual sighs, as if they're saying let it go. This schoolhouse is out of my hands. As the poet T.S. Eliot wrote, "Houses live and die."

But there are other places that still have a fighting chance. The skills we are cultivating in our life together are a way of strengthening the net in the larger community. The city is a bizarre river of humanity whose floodplain claims a little more land each spring. But even floodplains have an innate sense. If it is true that sprawl is by design (unorganized, of disparate groups, but still by design) rather than a lack of one, then our response needs to rise up from our communities. What Wendell Berry calls, "Complex local culture. . . . I mean the complex, never-completed affection for our land and our neighbors that is true patriotism."

Recently a few neighbors, "the communist" Brett included, started a group called Friends of the Rum River. Fifteen people showed up at the first meeting, and the number one concern voiced by all was unplanned development. As we walked along the riverbank gathering trash out of the tall grasses and among the trees, I talked with my neighbors. Shelley described the woodlands cooperative she recently started with private landowners who will sell sustainably harvested timber from their lands. Ken, a farmer and landowner, explained how farmers could reduce fertilized run-off and grow better crops by having their soil tested and using just the right amount of nutrients for their land. Eric's experience on the township board revealed that parceling off land in small lots with low end dwellings, which seems like a lucrative method, actually depletes the tax base so that neighbors end up subsidizing this kind of development. And when a high school teacher described the excitement of his students taking water samples from and writing stories about the river, I felt this strange sensation rising up in me. Buried so long beneath the outrage, it took me a while to realize that what I was feeling was hope. The first event scheduled for Friends of the Rum: to throw a party by the river.

At home later, I walked down to the river and watched a beaver swimming in a slow easy circle. As the sun settled on the water, I planned the ideal party—a rural Minnesotan's version of Babette's Feast—the best hot dishes full of cheese and noodles and soup and vegetables, imbued with the love and wisdom of the hands that taught these church recipes; and from the Ojibwe still in the area, steamed wild rice and pan-fried walleye and warm fry bread with maple syrup. All the people who might be moving up here from the Cities are there, as well as the spirits of those who came before us, the Dakota, Ojibwe, Voyageurs, Dutch, Norwegians and Swedes. Kids swim and tube in the river, fishermen throw in a line, and the neighbors visit. Like Babette's feast, something transformative happens, due to the beauty of the river and the nirvanic effect of consuming so much cholesterol and protein, causing heart valves to sluice and oxygen to slow to the brain, so that we are all in a tantric state of suspension.

Then the Spirit of the Rum River rises up from the dark water. Dressed in a mossy number, she has flowers woven through her hair. Spreading out her green skirt she sits on the bank, offers us glasses of Rum-water, and teaches us how to say her real name, Mde Wakan, Dakota for "Spirit River." She tells us funny stories about the early days of the river and her laughter is like water rippling over stones. We are feeling quite warm and happy when she takes us by the hand and we fly downstream, and she shows us the future of the Rum: suburban homes replace farmland; manicured lawns and smooth tarred drives fill in wetlands; trees are cut down for better views and messy brush and cattails eliminated for walking paths and permanent docks. We fly past charming verandas and bears carved out of stumps and cement deer feeding on white marble rocks with grinning gnomes underfoot. Rum River Estates, Riverview Homes, Rumshire Commons.

As we perch in a tree she shows us the flood of 2020, when the river, in all its rum-fury, will rise up and claim its plains, and there won't be wetlands to absorb its waters, and no one will argue about whether the land where their house is floating is technically a floodplain. We ask the good Spirit, "Is this a vision of what could be or what will be?" Spreading her ghostly arms over all of us, she says, "It is up to you."

And as we settle on the bank by the river, everyone sees vividly their place in the natural community. Farmers find new ways of staying small and working with the land. Families that thought they wanted to move out here realize, before they throw up a house, dig in the septic, pave in a drive, cut down the trees for a view and fertilize the new lawn down to the river, that they prefer to stay in the city and come up for visits. And others who still choose to move up build smaller houses closer to existing homes and further away from the water.

The Spirit is alive and moving through us so that we barely murmur surprise when Fyodor Dostoevsky appears on the riverbank in his rumpled dark suit and speaks to us in Russian, which we all understand as if he is merely reading the words written on our hearts:

It's a spiritual, psychological process. To transform the world, to recreate it afresh, men must turn into another path psychologically. Until you have become really, in actual fact, a brother to everyone, brotherhood will not come to pass. No sort of scientific teaching, no kind of common interest, will ever teach men to share property and privileges with equal consideration for all. Everyone will think his share too small and they will be always en-vying, complaining and attacking one another. You ask when it will come to pass; it will come to pass, but first we have to go through the period of isolation.

The period of isolation. We nod, grateful for the words to describe what we have been enduring. Then Mde Wakan and Fyodor announce the end of this pe-riod of isolation. A loud cheer rises up and we make a toast in honor of its passing. Mde Wakan describes how, long ago, from Mille Lacs Lake to Princeton there were so many trees the sun never hit the forest floor, and to the south was rolling prairie. Together, she suggests, if we were to tend to the forests we have, plant more, and restore the prairie, then we could cool the earth's fever and, motioning for us to come closer so that we all lean in to hear, she tells us what some of her people believe. If all the plants and soils are restored and the insects return, then so would the animals who once moved through these forests and prairies.

We place our hands together and agree to give away some of our acreage in order to bring back the forests and the prairie. The donated land is so vast it links up with property owned by the Mille Lacs Band of Ojibwe. Working with the tribe we will tear down unnecessary fences, dig up roads, and seed and plant the land. We will burn the prairie when needed and wait, in the wild and wondrous hope that our children's children's children may watch the elk and bison roam and hear the throaty boom of the prairie chickens. And with the help of our ancestors, our great great grandchildren, and the land that is our home, we will move closer to understanding what it means to live together.

Many thanks to the Blacklock Nature Sanctuary and the East Central Arts Council for their support.

Henry Bird and the
Dogs of Bogus Brook

(2007)

Henry Bird died. He was eighty-six. I study his face in the *Princeton Eagle* obituary: blue eyes, steady gaze, mouth parted in a smile. Henry is survived, among others, by a sister with the last name Fox. Bird. Fox.

Six winters ago I was driving my Subaru home from the repair shop in Princeton and was gathering speed on the first long stretch on County Road 4 when the engine died. I steered the car near the edge of the road before it stopped. It was dusk and what remained of the sun was in my eyes. I turned the hazards on and walked through the snow to the closest farm house—dark, no smoke—then cut across the cornfield and treeline to find an old man stacking wood. Before I called out, I took in the way he placed the logs, the years of experience reflected in his well-stacked woodpile. With his lined face, tan jacket and cap, he reminded me of a piece of wood. He looked up, glanced at my car, assessed the setting sun, and motioned for me to follow him into his house. "I'm Henry, that's Marie," he said, nodding to his wife, who had thick glasses and kept washing dishes at the sink, the smell of dinner lingering in their house.

Henry and I walked out in the cold toward the road. The sun had set and I heard the sound of a truck gaining velocity then braking as its headlights beamed on the dark presence of my car. We watched it swerve around then speed on.

In our intentional cul-de-sac, animals seem to find us. Millie the white German shepherd was left as a pup by Dana's woodshop, sick and near death, and now she's a senior with a bad hip. Sylvester the barncat showed up the first winter, when my husband Jeff and I were sharing the farmhouse with Jim and Debbie and their son Miles. The cat was a sack of black fur shivering on our porch and staring at us through the windows. Like a feline Mona Lisa, its green eyes found me in the kitchen and living room and hallways. We agreed not to feed it so it would go away, but one below-zero-wicked-cold morning I couldn't stand it, and I put out a bowl of dog chow. The cat leapt and devoured it like some crazed cartoon character. Sylvester settled into the barn and is still there, eleven years later.

Once we saw a bear. Dana and I were in the driveway discussing siding on the garage and then he hollered "Bear!" and ran toward the horse pasture, waving his arms at the brown-black creature that lumbered toward us then veered off into the patch of woods behind the farmhouse. We watched it scurry along the property line like it had been stung, which it might have by the electric fence. One July Fourth, when our friends camp out and we build fires and play guitars and sing and stay up too late, a white dove settled on Cyndy and Dana's roof. They named her Lovey. I had to mentally shrug off a lifetime of Jesus pictures and Hallmark cards to *see* this snowy, red-ring-eyed bird. When we had a picnic and dance on the back deck, Lovey would flit from one rooftop to another, and then tuck her head in like she was listening to our music and laughter. She left like she came, when we were looking the other way.

Neighbors' animals show up. A cross between a Weimariner and Rottweiler barreled past our screen doors and cleaned out bowls before we registered it as a non-compound dog. One evening Dana was alone out in the wood-fired hot tub. He was enjoying the fog which was hanging low to the ground, and the sun streaking orange in the horizon, and he screamed as a dark form bolted by him. A miniature pony, with burrs clotting its mane and tail, ducked under the fence and settled into graze near the three horses, where she stayed for a day or so until the neighbors showed up with truck and trailer.

Henry tried the engine, put it in neutral and told me to steer. I heard a grunt then turned to see he was pushing my car with his slight old frame. I cranked the wheel and the Subaru settled in gravel. Henry dropped in the passenger seat, clutched his chest and took raggedy breaths as he said, "Give me a minute. Just back from Mayo. Farmed all my life, then the heart started acting up, they can't figure out the problem."

"Henry!" I felt a pain in my own chest as I braced against the door, sure he was going to die. How was I going to explain letting an eighty-year-old man push my car? And how did I not know CPR? "Should I call 911?"

He waved that away. We sat and I breathed with him, then it seemed like his heart found the right track. "I'll give you a lift home," he said.

As we drove down County 4 in his minivan we talked about living around here. He and his first wife Hope moved to the farm in 1961. I asked him if he knew about the dances that started up again at the Dalbo Town Hall, with string bands and a caller. "Marie doesn't care much for dancing. Hope and I used to love to dance, especially polka. Danced for thirty years together."

When he pulled into our gravel drive, the dogs circled the van, and Millie jumped up on his door. "Sorry, Henry, it's not my dog. I might have to call you later. I'm worried about your heart. Are you in the phonebook? What's your last name?"

"Bird." His blue eyes took in the farmhouse, gazed up at Dana and Cyndy peering down from the window of the renovated garage, over at the lights of the straw bale house, and then briefly settled on me. "Henry Bird. Call if you need to, but I'll be alright."

Animals reveal their humans. My neighbor and sister-in-law Diane bought a black lab pup from someone at the hospital where she's a nurse. She wanted so much for her kids to wake up Christmas morning to find a squirming bundle under the tree, and that's how Lucy came into our lives. Those first weeks it was hard to stay away from their farmhouse: Lucy was cuddly, dark-eyed, pink-tongued puppy cute. As she grew she started to limp and one thousand dollars later she was humping around on a cast, and a few months further in sweet little Lucy turned into Lucifer—a slathering crooked-leg adolescent shouldering through our screen doors, jumping vertically to turn door handles, nosing lids off metal trash cans of dog food, and tunneling a path under our compost box so all the dogs could chow down on our scraps.

When we weren't home Lucy would come in, grab a shoe and run off. For a few days we'd search the house then maybe stumble over it at night on our way to the dumpster or the neighbors. Something about struggling to identify this laceless, mauled, dirt-encrusted object stirred existential anxiety. The shoe became a hook caught on the lower extremities of Being. Merrells, Sorrels, and Clarks, carefully chosen—"Does this rub on my heel? Make my feet look big? Keep my toes warm in fifteen below?"—all leveled in the jaws of Lucifer. You found yourself in the dark asking, Is this my shoe? How did it get here? Who am I? What does it matter?

One day I came out of the back door to the cries of my five-year-old. I rushed over to Brett and Diane's lawn to see Franny sobbing as Lucy nipped her, her big paws landing on Franny's back, boing – boing. I kicked at the dog, looked accusingly at the house, picked Franny up who was hiccupping and breathless, and I thought all the bad thoughts I kept away and stored up unknowingly.

Later, Diane came over with a bouquet of flowers from her garden and a sorry letter to Franny. Lucy trotted along and we gave her a bone.

Which reminds me of the community photo we took a few years into living here. It was early in the morning, below freezing; our wee little kids were wrapped in blankets and caps and buttoned into our coats. I was trying to enjoy this moment of togetherness but it was cold and I was tired from staying up late the night before, and I had made cinnamon rolls, which were warm and waiting for us on the picnic table while we positioned ourselves on hay bales in the open part of the barn where the wind can really gather up the incline of meadows. After several photos, fingers, and faces were freezing and kids were squirming, and when I hopped down to get the pan of rolls I discovered the dogs had eaten all but the crust of two. Blame it on my Romanian-Italian genes but I hate the cold and still, after eleven years in Minnesota, I have to talk myself out of taking it as a personal affront, so I was looking forward to the warm comfort of melted icing mingling with cinnamony bread. Anger and resentment. Mumbled apologies. Animals and humans.

The neighbors who are quiet have a cat who is a wild panther stalking songbirds, peeing on plants in gardens and terrorizing children by crouching behind bushes and pouncing on them. The neighbors who are organized have a dog that jumps on people and leaves scratches on car doors. The neighbor who is me has a beagle that humps other female dogs and startles the horses by getting underfoot and barking that shrill piercing call

We take turns being surprised that they don't do more. We take turns feeling superior and judgmental and humbled and ashamed. Animals remind us who we are and reveal more of who our neighbors are, and we are better for the knowing. Living in community, this is a good thing to remember, because you find at times you wish your neighbor to be different. More industrious or communal, or less. You discover an internal list of qualities a friend and neighbor should have that you don't realize you carry around until they disappoint you. Animals are a valve for parts of ourselves we'd rather keep hidden. Our responses to events come from a chaotic jumble of feelings and experiences that look the opposite of Henry Bird's neat log pile. It's not just a roll or a shoe, it's the feelings we bury, disappointments that take a lifetime to cultivate, the awareness of how hard it is to really live with other humans. Not just coexist and wave when you are both out in your lawns or pulling into the drive, or seeing each other in a planned way—when you are showered and the house is picked up and you have a glass of wine in hand—but when the neighbor's dog has dug a hole in your flower garden and snapped off the Liseanthus which was about to bloom, or when the neighbor's horse has eased past the fencing and is munching on your seeded young grass and leaving dark mounds of gratitude.

It's a given, taking responsibility for your animals. That aside, disappointment is your own hairshirt. Friends and neighbors press into it, but when you examine your flesh wounds you are studying the imprint of your own life.

That night I lay in bed mentally willing Henry to stay alive. The next day I looked him up in the phonebook and called and no one answered, which confirmed for me that he was in the ICU at Princeton Hospital. The girls and I made chocolate chip oatmeal bars and I knocked on his door with a plate and a card. Around Henry's last name I had drawn a crane with its wings extended. I was thinking of Marquez' title, "A Very Old Man with Enormous Wings."

Marie appeared.

"Good morning. How's Henry?"

"He's laying down."

I handed her the bars through the part of the screen door she opened. "I worried he strained himself yesterday. I didn't know he was going to push the car. It was really nice of him to help me."

She looked down. Her glasses made her eyes swimmy and small. We stood there. "He helps a lot of people, but most don't think to thank him, or come around, unless they need something."

I considered this comment and decided it was an acknowledgement of sorts. After a decade of living here it is still hard for me to decipher the ways of the mostly Scandinavian and Dutch neighbors. I feel like an Irish Setter in a room full of military personnel. I don't understand their tacit code and they look askance at the slobber I leave on their uniforms. Marie nodded at my girls in their car seats, and then closed the door.

From then on, when I drove up and down County Road 4, Henry Bird's place became part of my focus of attention. I would study the pumpkin-stained farmhouse and garage, surrounded on three sides by cornfields. Often Henry was outside wearing the same cap and jacket, stacking wood or working in their flower garden—a narrow rectangle of dark soil with rows of gladiolas, geraniums, begonias, and dahlias trailing up white trellises. If he was there I felt more at ease in the world. If the house was dark, I pressed the gas pedal and continued down County 4, ruminating on my life and wondering about Henry's.

I drive up and down County 4 a lot. It is part of my

trek to Minneapolis to teach at the university. On a good day it takes me an hour and a half one way. I ought to be thrown in environmental prison. An eco-penitentiary, imagine.

—What were you in for?

—Driving too much. Building a dwelling that could house five refugee families, moving out to the country, hence complicit in the urban march. Living as a North American.

—What was your sentence?

—Untangling the Gordian knot of desire and consumption.

Sometimes Wendell Berry appears in the passenger side of my mind, casting a stark light on my choices. "The thing is Wendell," I say, "I have a good job and can't find anything closer. I wasn't heedless along the way. I made each choice mindfully, first marriage, then community, then the land, then the kids came along, then the house to put them in and the cars to get to the jobs which fund the rest. Each decision is like a padded ring around me and the fabric of these choices has created an astronaut suit necessary for me to orbit Working and Married with Children in the Middle Way."

Wendell looks sidelong at me as a fish would, or a prophet, then he gazes out the window at spew from the mouth of the giant named Commerce. Over the years

Wendell and I have watched Commerce's northward reach through wetlands, forests and fields. Banks go in first, always. As Brecht said, "What is breaking into a bank compared with founding a bank?"

Only at the tail end of my return trip home does it start to feel like country, and when I drive along County 4 the afternoon light reflects off barns and silos and the flat expanse of fields: corn stubble and pocks of soil on white planes, or green shoots in dark rows. I let out a breath I didn't know I was holding and recall the ancient exchange between land and sky. I consider how they mirror each other, as if the fields are an artist's rendering of the sky, and the farms are mere clouds.

Like mind-fingers moving along rosary beads, or a *lectio divina* of the land, this is what County Road 4 has become for me. Among the treelines and fields is the Johnsons' dairy farm with round hay bales stacked differently than other neighbors—placed on the flat ends then a top row of bales on their curved sides like a roof— and two rows of these spaced apart so that there is a tunnel big enough for a tractor to pass through. There's the faded one-room schoolhouse that seems to be deep in thought about its own slow collapse. Up a slight incline is Wendell Hill cemetery, established 1899. Sometimes I go to the rise and gaze out at the corn and soy bean fields, the barns and houses, the lone old tree in the near field. I study the gravestones, reading the names of the dead—*Johnson, Oquist, Lindquist, Larsen*—my eyes settling on the soil of a freshly dug grave.

On to the farm with the grey donkey called Whisper. He looks like a miniature lead toy that a child places here and there: donkey staring at fence, donkey backed up to faded blue barn, donkey next to horse near hay. Along the river is the neighbor we buy pumpkins from every fall, next to the Bogus Brook Township Hall where we vote. Crossing the bridge I look out over the Rum River. This wild river, constant and changing, where we've canoed, swam, skied, fished, floated, camped and hiked along, is a liquid current powering the countryside.

Now and again when I cross the river and a car is approaching from the opposite direction, I flash back to when the young driver went left of center and crashed into Jim and Debbie's car. They were on their way to church where Debbie is a pastor and she was reading over her sermon. Miles was in the carseat in the back. The impact split their car in two. The neighbors we buy pumpkins from ran out of their house at the unearthly screech and helped Jim and Debbie. Remarkably, all ended up fine. This memory and others from time past—a horse standing on the double yellow line, a drunk man in the snowy ditch struggling to open his car door in the dark—and much further back in time—glacial movement revealed in the rises and dips, the marshes and bogs, the stands of birch, maple, cottonwoods, and aspen, as well as the clusters of white pines that used to dominate the land before logging and farming—are contained in time present for me on County Road 4.

In June each summer a neat hand-painted sign for tomatoes appeared in Henry's yard. Though we have tomatoes spilling off the porch and gathering flies in the kitchen, I stopped and bought some. I admired his gleaming silver Airstream parked behind the garage; sometimes Marie was working in the garden with a scarf over her hair. About three years ago a painted sign appeared in the yard in Henry's old man style, "Airstream for Sale." Before I even had a chance to try on that dream with Jeff, our farming friends bought it from Henry and placed it on a knoll overlooking the Rum River. My friend told me this Airstream was what Henry and his first wife Hope traveled in for years. They covered forty-eight of the fifty states. Inside the Airstream everything was preserved—homemade linens and curtains, silverware, cups, dishes—a shrine to Henry and Hope's life together. In a drawer my friend discovered a packet of letters between Henry and Hope, perhaps when he served in the Coast Guard in World War II. She returned them to Henry unread.

I thought about Henry living his life with his wife Marie, working in the garden, sharing meals and the dark eternal evenings of Minnesota winter. And the Airstream parked just outside, homage to his life with Hope, dancing, raising children, and traveling the states. And I wondered, when Henry was tilling soil or stacking wood, did he ever pause and find himself moving to the Airstream? Did he take a moment from the present to reenter his former life, or was it enough to know it was there? And what were his feelings when he made the decision to sell the Airstream?

There are different kinds of happiness.

"So, there's a horse you want me to kill?" Rob asks me during our first conversation. I call him on his cell phone as he's driving from Montana with all of his possessions in a U-Haul. He's an old friend of Brett's and he's moving to our farm to live in Brett and Diane's house and take care of their animals for the year they will be living in New Zealand.

"What?"

"My cousin said you have a sick horse, cancer or a

tumor, and she thought it would be nice if I took care of it for you."

"Geez, what kind of a place you think we are? 'Welcome to the farm, hope you have a rifle, there's the old grey mare, or in Whinny's case the gelding.' No, the vet's going to come out and put it down. Don't worry."

He sounds relieved. "'Cause I'd rather not. And I wouldn't want the kids to associate Whinny's death with me."

Rob settles into our intentional cul-de-sac. He's about our age which is a relief because anyone younger would serve as another reminder of how old we all are. He gets along great with the kids, and his big mutt fits in fine.

The vet drives out, says Whinny can live this way for a while, but that we'll want to bury him before the ground freezes, and deep enough so the animals can't dig him up. Or we can pay to have him carted away. I think its good the vet's going to take care of it as none of us own a gun. We live on the land with animals, but we don't live in a way that makes us familiar with the methods of putting an end to life.

With a shovel Rob starts digging a hole behind the barn, beyond where we buried the dogs. He could use a backhoe but he seems to enjoy the task; to go out there when he feels like it, his progress visible. When the dairy farmer from the adjacent property comes over to see if he can pheasant hunt on our side of the line, we ask him how he disposes of his dead cows. He buries them in wood shavings and lye. They decompose quickly, he says, but we know not always because now and again our dogs will trot across our yards, heads high, carrying a bone straight out of Flintstones or a cow skull with flaps of hide and cartilage bouncing along. I like to observe the stir in the dog clan, the bone-bearer proud, protective, the other dogs pacing around her, waiting for the chance to move in.

Some tasks here are divided along gender lines. The men shovel and grade the road, mow the path through the meadows and along the river, and in this case, deal with Whinny's death. I am relieved to let them while I tend to the kids, the house, and teaching. I occasionally wander over and scratch the horse's noses and the girls give them hay, but mostly the horses are part of the landscape my eyes settle on through the day. Part of the beauty.

One day Franny, now six, comes home from playing with Louis next door. She is wearing her favorite paisley brown skirt with a polka dot shirt and a pink headband. While she names the seeds she planted in pots with Louis and Cyndy, in my mind I finally locate what her voice reminds me of—the mourning doves that settled on my bedroom window sill when I was growing up—low and throaty. I notice that Franny's blue eyes don't occupy so much of her face, that she has gone from a fleshy toddler to a long-legged girl. I go back to washing dishes and ask her what else she and Louis did. "Played Pokémon cards, put pretty rocks and flowers on Whinny's grave. Only that made us remember Fargo and feel sad."

My hands stop wiping a plate. "But the grave is empty, right? You put stones and flowers around the hole?"

"Whinny's dead. He's in the grave." Franny eyes me as if registering that she knows a life and death matter that I don't.

I call Cyndy, who tells me that the day before, Rob decided to take the matter in his own hands. He called on Dana who agreed to assist him. Debbie adds what she knows, which includes a rifle borrowed from the dairy farmer, two shots, and a struggle to maneuver the body in the hole. I call Rob and it is hard for him to talk about it because it ended up being a bigger deal than he thought. He wanted to save Brett and Diane money, and he wanted it not to be traumatic for any of us, especially the kids, so he did it under the radar.

Once I got over the irony that what Rob didn't want to happen, happened at his own hands, this incident revealed an aspect of life in community: there is no under the radar. The truth outs itself. Children are lower to the ground and live among the animals and notice death and honor it. They have held services for a flattened desiccated chipmunk, and baby mice and rabbits and birds that Olivia rescues from her cat's jaws, which suffered, died, and got buried. If something significant happens in someone's life we find out, not in a gossipy way, or if it is, in that sense of the word that Kathleen Norris refers to in *Dakota* where the knowledge knits us together. What we need to know seems to secrete from our collective pores. Even if no one uttered a word the news would bubble up from the banana peels and coffee grounds in our compost heap.

We can't hide the truth even if we try, and this is a good thing. It reanimates the question that cycles back through my life in which I have lived like a fox skirting the watchful eye of first Catholicism, then Evangelicalism: What is so bad about the truth?

It's tempting to think that you would be different if you lived by friends on a piece of land. You and your animals and children (what goes for animals goes for kids) would stay within respectable boundaries, that not so much of you would leak out like ink from a broken pen, but something primitive and inescapable emerges about humans living in fenceless proximity. Life with friends, like marriage and family, is shaped by a desire to know and be known, and there are those inevitable moments of not knowing and feeling not known. The moments when you venture beyond the public gaze and navigate failure.

Through the failed moments and the day-to-day living, staying put with these people in this place is for me, oddly, akin to brushing the hem of God. As Mae West put it, "I knew that in some marvelous way I had touched the hem of the unknown. And being me, I wanted to lift that hemline a little bit more." Perhaps it's the sacramentalism I learned at an early age, but I desire glimpses of the divine in my living, and find them in my backyard. For someone who has spent much of her adult life moving every two years, there is something of the divine in continuing to find good reasons to stay put, with friends and family.

Given the times, I am reluctant to talk about my faith. To admit to being a Christian turns me into an unwilling magician. I say "Jesus" and voilà, a black hat appears in my hand which produces white doves and crosses and political agendas touted as Christian truths, and the biggest trick of them all—Christ holding a gun in one hand and an American flag in the other. Non. Nyet. Nein. The rise in Christian fundamentalism has led me to feel at times that the best thing I could do as a believer is never say a word. A twist on the vow of silence. But to leave God out would be like omitting that we live along the wild Rum River—a sensuous dynamic element informing the ground of my being. These encounters with my neighbors make me recognize my need, and somehow grace is essential in my ability to see my need. When I realize my own inability to love adequately or to be my ideal, it is given to me to see. The grace is there in the seeing.

What is essential will be revealed.

Which brings me to judgment. Judgments grow like buckthorn in community. I judge and I am judged. The judgments are mostly subterranean thoughts involving bikes and balls slewn here and there and missing tools and lights kept on at night and how fast you drive and pets ("You're getting another cat? Dog?"), to deeper issues of parenting, money-spending, and how we interact (or don't) with each other.

This came as a shock to me, for I believe judgment is responsible for much of the world's misery. Growing up Catholic and having experienced the back hand of judgment against my brothers, I tried to live out, "Judge not lest ye be judged." I ingested Kierkegaard's words, "Purity of heart is to will one thing," in order to remove judgment from my heart and to live in a way that would not incur any from others. I was in the first grade, playing with the neighbor kids in our front yard, when the bully turned my big brother upside down and shoved his nose in a pile of dog crap. I turned forty-three when reports from Abu Ghraib started surfacing. From the individual to the collective, judgment lies at the core of suffering. According to Buddhist scripture, "Everything that we are is the result of what we have thought" says *The Dhammapada.* Thought begets judgment which begets action which shapes reality. Mental fences contain and vilify the other, the outcast. Some people live as if their judgments are all they have. Many occupy positions in our current government administration. Hell, in my opinion, would be the inability to experience any life apart from our judgments.

I have met only three people who seem to have excised judgment: a Carmelite nun, a friend in the last stages of AIDS, and a woman who dropped so much acid her eyes were that stainless blue you only see in hardcore alcoholics. She spent most of her time playing a violin on the beach. What unites these three is the extremity required to dwell in a place beyond judgment. Living among friends has expunged hopes of being one of them, and for me that's a step toward freedom.

What I've come to accept is not only the incessant, DNA-encoded, seemingly necessary part of survival judgment plays, but also how little substance our judgments really have. Something good comes of living past my mental assertions and finding them wrong, or when they are right, they're not painted in the harsh colors of my personal palette of fear, insecurity, and anger. Time and again I've unwittingly marshaled these shock troops of complaints against my neighbor, and then he fixes my birdhouse or plays basketball with my kids, or she feeds me when I'm having low blood sugar, and surprises me by making me laugh when I'm in my own hell. For me it is a kind of freedom to accept I will be judged. I've come to see that judgments are sticks tossed in the river, carried away by the current of living, and that creates hope.

We need more hope, don't we? Because we still live in the paradox of judgment, that what has little weight can also perpetuate genocide and oppression. Given the relentless scapegoating by both individuals and society, the notion of stringing up the Divine continues to hold relevance for me. If judgment is society's mud line, then freedom from judgment is why I continue to have faith. The word "Christ" is a kind of Alakazam! What pops out of the black hat this time is the rabbit of misconception that all Christians believe that Christianity is the One True Way. I see the world's holy persons as lakes—Jesus, the Buddha, Krishna, Rabia, Lao-Tze, Sophia, Black Elk—shimmering portals of True Being. Seen from the sky, the light shining off of the water reflects love and mercy for enemies and neighbors.

What keeps me dwelling in the mysterious depths of Christianity is the hope that in his death, Christ takes on both our need to judge as well as the devastating impacts of our judgments. Through the crucifixion, it is as if the legal grounds for rendering judgment against us have been dismissed from our cases. Judging even ourselves is deemed null and void, for mercy's sake. Even praise or public acclaim, which after all is only a judgment in the affirmative, is no longer relevant. And through the resurrection, somehow, remarkably, (and many will call me a magician for believing this), the presence of the divine becomes more real, more with us, and forgiveness and unity replace division. Though the violent aspect in our natures will continue to bear it away, on some elemental level, what was done is undone, and where there was judgment there is grace, and grace is what animates us and gives us breath—*nefesh*. Life among friends, at times mirrors this movement from judgment to grace. My mental declarations against my neighbors are extinguished by the experience of living with them, of being renewed by who they are now, today, in the flesh.

After reading Henry's obituary I got in my car and drove along County 4 toward his place. I noted the For Sale signs and the new houses where there used to be fields and recalled old farmers. John and Sylvia, one of the original Dutch families who owned the dairy farm next to us, came to our open house ten years ago. Sylvia brought red gladiolas from her garden. The couple was well into their seventies then, and passed the farm on to their grandson. I remembered the group of older farmers who gathered under the white pines of a nearby dairy farm to talk with Senator Paul Wellstone just a few months before he died. They asked Wellstone questions about market prices, yield, subsidies, and legislation. When I thought about these farmers and the collective knowledge required to make a living from the land, it is as if the wheel of life became visible, and Henry's death marked the turning of the wheel. I pulled into his drive; the house was dark. As I wondered about what might happen to Marie, I looked over the garden at the birdhouse Henry made, and just outside my window, his painted wood cut of a John Deere tractor and driver with a cap like Henry's, mounted on his mailbox. The driver looked happy riding that tractor.

Henry, where do the dead go? What is it like in a place beyond disappointment and judgment, beyond the burdens that come along with different kinds of happiness? Are you with Hope?

When I drove home, I turned onto our gravel drive and glanced out at the row of white pines growing along the property line. They were government plugs planted when we moved here eleven years ago, and they've matured enough to hold back some of the snow drifts from the field. The drive curved along our house, and straightened to Brett and Diane's farmhouse, with its wrap-around porch and swing. Between our places was the garden in its late summer decline, sunflowers reckless and brave. I looked over at Dana and Cyndy's renovated barn and garage, with the red wood siding and white trim, and Jim and Debbie's straw bale house beyond, and I drove slowly along our yards scattered with wood piles, bikes, and children. I have seen these things countless times, but what was new in this moment, what I most noticed, was the light striking the wagging tails of the dogs—white, black, brown, swish-swish—by the tractor, on the porch, and in the drive. This gracious welcoming motion is repeated many times every day, like strokes of a clock, and it was revealed to me on this day, this part of the invisible art that shapes our lives.

Acknowledgments

The East Central Arts Council for support through grants. The Blacklock Nature Sanctuary Fellowship, the New York Mills Cultural Center, and the Ragdale Foundation for support through residencies.

Debbie Blue, Cyndy Rudolph, Leah Buturain, Pete Hedberg, Brett Larson, and William D. Adamson for close reading and generous feedback.

Dan Hoisington at Cathedral Hill Press for making this book not only possible, but also a life-giving venture.

The International Crane Foundation for bringing us together one bird at a time.

Malvina Reynolds, whose song, "This World's Gone Beautiful," was the inspiration for the title.

My neighbors and friends, who tolerate me telling stories about them.

My mother Rita and father John, who helped me to find the wonder of the stories in our lives.

My sister Leah, muse and constant friend.

My brothers Mark and JD, for your presence.

All of my relatives for your love and support.

Jeff, Audrey, and Frances, without whom the world would never have gone beautiful.